Partners

in

Independence

Partners

in

Independence

A Success Story of Dogs and the Disabled

Ed and Toni Eames

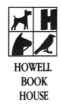

HOWELL
BOOK
HOUSE

New York

Howell Book House

A Simon and Schuster Macmillan Company

1633 Broadway

New York, NY 10019

Library of Congress Cataloging-in-Publication Data

Eames, Edwin.

    Partners in independence: a success story of dogs and the disabled / Ed and Toni Eames.

    p. cm.

  ISBN 0-87605-595-1

    1. Guide dogs. 2. Human-animal relationships. I. Eames, Toni.

II. Title.

HV1780.S4E25   1997

362.4'183--dc21   97-5992

                                     CIP

Manufactured in the United States of America

99 98 97 9 8 7 6 5 4 3 2 1

Book Design: Scott Meola

Cover Design: Scott Meola

Cover Photo: David Pollack / The Stock Market

To our beloved animals who have so enriched our lives and to the thousands of devoted dogs who have brought greater independence to their disabled partners, this book is gratefully dedicated.

CONTENTS

FOREWORD

I first met Ed and Toni Eames at the 1995 Dog Writers Association of America (DWAA) banquet in New York City, which takes place each year the night before the Westminster Kennel Club dog show. As president of DWAA, it is my privilege to present awards to the outstanding dog writers selected by the judges of each category. Ed and Toni received a first place award, a Maxwell medallion for the article they wrote about "Kirby," Ed's three-legged guide dog. The following year they received top honors for their column, "Partners in Independence," which appears in *Dog World* magazine. Ed and Toni have carved out a niche in the dog writing world focusing on the relationship between people with disabilities and their canine assistants. As you read this book, you will enter their unique domain and share it with an audience that extends well beyond the dog-loving community. By the way, Ed and Toni are both blind.

I was young and impressionable when I first thought about what it meant to live without sight. My new interest was the result of a movie I saw about a blind writer who solves a murder case with the help of his guide dog. When I got home from the movie, I decided to satisfy my curiosity about how my world would be without sight. I pulled the shades, closed my eyes, and the world as I knew it changed. I lost my bearings, tripped and fell, badly frightening myself. As a result, I never again played games requiring a blindfold.

Most of us have not been in a position to observe the relationship between disabled human and assistance dog. As Ed and Toni continuously suggest in all that they write, this relationship is a partnership based on mutual trust, aid, support and bonding. For that reason, *Partners in Independence* is the perfect title for this book as well as for their *Dog World* column. With the knowledge and eloquence derived from being insiders, they take us into the everyday lives of their peers. We not only read about the heroic hearing dog who saved her deaf partner from being injured by a falling tree limb and the service dog who brought the portable phone to his partner when he fell out of a wheelchair, but also about dogs who have increased the independence of their human partners and improved the quality of their lives in less spectacular ways. It's the everyday activities of helping a blind partner cross a road, a deaf partner know the telephone is ringing and a physically disabled partner by picking up a dropped item, that the true "miracle" unfolds.

Ed and Toni will take you by the hand, as they took me, on a bright journey into a world I thought was remote and unknowable, and to be honest, a bit frightening. The authors not only show us the upside of partnership with assistance dogs, but the downside as well. Things we rarely think about—matches not working out, early retirement of canine partners, the financial burden of working with a dog—are explored in depth. It is a pleasure to delve into a book that is so informative, wide-ranging, emotional and well-written. I hope you will enjoy exploring the world of canine assistants and their human partners as much as I have.

At the end of this odyssey, you will come to know many of the people the authors know, the places they've been, and the special way they experienced it all. You too will laugh, cry and think. You will also come away with the surprising understanding that there is no such place as "the world of the disabled." There is only the world and we all share it.

Mordecai Siegal

Mordecai Siegal is the President of the Dog Writers Association of America. He is the author of twenty-one books about dogs, cats and horses. His work has appeared in many national magazines, including *House Beautiful.*

ACKNOWLEDGMENTS

Over the years a number of people have been instrumental in assisting us with our *Dog World* columns. Melanie Whitesides and Norm Leventhal joined us in a brainstorming session resulting in our column name, Partners in Independence. We want to thank Micky Bergstrom, former editor of *Dog World*, for her foresight in contracting with us to write the column. Current *Dog World* editor Donna Marcel and her staff continue to encourage us to explore all aspects of the assistance dog field.

Several of our columns were made possible through generous travel grants from American Airlines. These grants enabled us to visit many assistance dog training programs and to make presentations at several veterinary schools.

We extend special appreciation to Alicia Bone, Philip Finnigan and Diane Anderson for lending their grammatical expertise to our columns. Although our voice-synthesized computer does an outstanding job in reading our initial drafts, we thank our many volunteer readers for lending a human voice to the re-reading and editing process.

Partners in Independence—the book—would not have been possible without the cooperation of the many programs and individuals featured herein. These folks, committed to furthering knowledge of the assistance dog movement, generously responded to our call for help by supplying the photographs needed for this book.

As blind writers, one of the most difficult tasks we faced was the selection of photographs for the book. Through our friendship network, we found Jean Harris, who became our photographic consultant. We extend our appreciation for the many hours she spent sifting through hundreds of pictures, describing them to us in detail and helping in the final selection process. We also thank Karen Newcomb for stepping in at the last minute to take several photographs to round out the pictorial coverage. Working with the staff of Avo's Lab in the conversion of our many color prints and slides into black and whites was a pleasant experience.

We extend special gratitude to our friends, Beth and Helen Shea, who edited the final manuscript. Beth, who is a night owl, kept us up into the wee hours making final corrections and suggestions.

We want to give particular recognition to our feline and canine family members. While we worked on this manuscript, Cameo spent many hours purring on Toni's lap. Kimmel never failed to notify us of meal times, his of course, not ours. Kizzy, with his Siamese antics, often reminded us that too much work and no play was not a proper way to run a household. To reinforce his message, he would occasionally stroll across the keyboard creating some weird and unintelligible messages from our voice synthesizer. Finally, our Golden Retriever guide dogs, Echo and Escort, bored with quietly lying around as we toiled at the computer, would occasionally take the opportunity to engage in a wrestling match in the tiny den where we worked. Not wanting to interfere with their fun, we simply turned up the volume on the voice output to override the noise of their grunts and growls.

To all who helped in this important project, human, canine and feline, our heartfelt and undying thanks.

Chapter One

First—Some Background

Where should two dog lovers hold their wedding? At the home of their veterinarian, of course. On June 14, 1987, our guide dogs, Perrier and Ivy, were the attendants at our wedding at the home of Dr. Gerald Tobias. After taking our marriage vows, Cantor Michael Loring officiated at a perpetual friendship ceremony for Ivy and Perrier. Among the seventy guests were three other guide dogs.

Perrier and Ivy serve as the attendants at the wedding of their partners, Ed and Toni Eames, held at the home of their veterinarian, Dr. Gerald Tobias.

Our wedding was the culmination of our first collaborative book effort. We met several years earlier when Ed was interviewing people partnered with guide dogs for a book he was writing about guide dog schools. At first Toni was an interviewee, then collaborator, then co-author and ultimately wife.

After our move to Fresno, California, we carved out a new career focused on dogs. Within the broad range of dog activities, we concentrated on the relationship between people with disabilities and the dogs who assist them.

Since February 1990, we have written a regular column for *Dog World* magazine. Our goal then, as it is now, was to inform the dog-loving public, as well as those interested in human interest stories, about the impact assistance dogs have on the lives of their disabled partners. The relationship between disabled person and assistance dog is a two-way street. Dogs help their human teammates and humans care for and nurture their canine assistants. In this book, we bring you accounts of dogs who have made a difference for some special humans and some humans who have provided meaningful lives for some special canines. Because this book is based on columns published from 1990 to 1995, the information reflects that time span.

Portrait of Toni

Despite my mother's admonitions to be cautious, I was one of those kids who had to pet every animal I could get my hands on. As a legally blind child with limited vision, this infatuation with furry things led to some embarrassing moments. On several occasions I reached out to cuddle what I perceived to be an animal, only to discover that it was a fur collar on a coat or the head of a crawling child.

My real love affair with dogs began at age five with my family's acquisition of a pet. Ginger, a small Terrier-Spaniel cross, remained part of our family until his death during my freshman year in college. In my senior year, I moved out of the college dormitory into my own apartment. Before getting furniture, I rushed to the nearest humane society to find a new canine companion. My new adoptee, Loki, a Shepherd-Terrier cross, was a spoiled brat until Charm, my first guide, entered our family. Being teamed with a guide dog stimulated my interest in becoming an outstanding dog handler and I used my newly acquired skills to convert Loki into a well-mannered pet.

Despite my love of all animals, particularly dogs, I was swayed by the anti-guide dog attitudes expressed by counselors, teachers and blind peers. Then in my early 20s I met several guide dog partners and was amazed at the variety of things these dogs could do. They stopped at curbs, located subway stairs, avoided obstacles, negotiated crowds, guided their partners to the door of an often-used restaurant and found an empty table. One day a friend and I met at the Port Authority bus terminal, one of the busiest, noisiest and most complex transportation hubs in New York City. I was astonished by his dog's skill in locating the ticket booth, the stairs to the upper level and the gate from which the bus left. He explained that this was not the feat of a miracle dog, but the response of a well-trained guide who had mastered a familiar route.

After that trip with my friend through the Port Authority, I was ready to trade my cane for a furry mobility device. Like most blind kids growing up in the 1950s, my training with a white cane did not begin until I was sixteen. Although the professionals said I was a competent cane user, I never felt comfortable with it. I felt insecure, vulnerable and very much alone.

In March 1967, I spent a month training with a Golden Retriever named Charm at Guiding Eyes for the Blind in Yorktown Heights, New York. Partnership with this Golden girl was one of the most significant turning points in my life. The following September, I began graduate school in the heart of New York City. With Charm as my guide, I could not believe how tension-free traveling had become. We used subways and buses, walked along unfamiliar streets, negotiated crowded thoroughfares and found our way to lecture halls, classrooms and the library. The first time Charm and I breezed through the Port Authority bus terminal with the same ease and proficiency demonstrated several months earlier by my friend and his dog was both a thrill and a milestone for me.

After receiving my master's degree, Charm was an integral partner in my search for a job. Like many blind people, I ran into employment discrimination. With my furry friend as emotional support, job interviews were less scary. On my way home from these ordeals, I could discuss my impressions with Charm before getting to a telephone to discuss my interview with a human friend. Charm was there to share the joy of landing my first job as a rehabilitation counselor at Kings Park Psychiatric Center (KPPC) in

Toni and her colleagues at Kings Park Psychiatric Center celebrate Charm's fifth birthday.

eastern Long Island. In fact, she was one of the reasons I was offered the job. My supervisor recognized the therapeutic impact of a dog on the lives of mentally ill patients long before there was documented evidence of this fact.

Charm's impact on my life was revolutionary. B.C. (Before Charm) I lacked confidence and had difficulty advocating on my own behalf. A.D. (After Dog) I became self-assured and spoke out for my rights. Charm became my alter ego. I took inordinate joy in her accomplishments and was acutely embarrassed by her mistakes. I had no intention of allowing school authorities, restaurant owners, theater managers and taxi drivers to deny access to my well-behaved, well-trained canine companion. Phrases like, "Get that dog out of here" and "No dogs allowed" made me angry enough to fight this rampant discrimination rather than reducing me to tears.

Charm's death in 1977 left my life in turmoil. I had never experienced such a devastating loss. Her successor, a Golden Retriever named Flicka, was so different in temperament it took months to learn to love her. Where Charm was calm and gentle, Flicka was rough and wild. They both had the impeccable manners of professional guides in harness, but Flicka was a dynamo when not on duty. For the seven years of our working partnership, Flicka and I lived and worked in New York.

In contrast to my first two guides, my third Golden, Ivy, split her working career between New York and California. When I married Ed, we gave up the hectic life of New York City commuters for the suburban routines of a small California city. Subway travel, incessantly honking car horns and congested sidewalks are memories to be revived during visits back to New York. Our relatively sedentary daily routines have been punctuated by exciting and busy trips to Israel, Bermuda, Canada, Mexico and more than twenty states.

All three of my Golden girls have successfully competed in American Kennel Club (AKC) Obedience Trials, with Ivy becoming the first guide dog to obtain the intermediate level title of Companion Dog Excellent (CDX). They have all been goodwill ambassadors for the guide dog movement with their impeccable public behavior and outstanding performance as guides. People are attracted to dogs and feel more comfortable speaking with those of us partnered with guide dogs. I enjoy these unsolicited contacts and have met and befriended many interesting people through the canine connection.

When not in harness, Flicka takes on the role of therapy dog with patients at Kings Park Psychiatric Center where Toni was employed as a rehabilitation counselor.

Just before Ivy's twelfth birthday she was diagnosed with a retinal disease rapidly causing loss of vision. Understandably, this was a great blow. We all wish for the immortality of those people and animals we love and rely on, even though we are fully aware that this wish can never be granted. Life with animals can be a particularly poignant cycle of love and loss. As I lost Ivy as my guide, her successor, Escort, came into my life.

Escort, my first male Golden guide, was trained at Leader Dogs for the Blind in Rochester, Michigan. His delightful personality and responsible guiding style have already brought me great happiness and he is a worthy successor to my three Golden girls.

Portrait of Ed

Unlike Toni, my adventure with guide dogs began much later in life. In fact, my romance with Toni was based upon my romance with guide dogs.

In 1972, at the age of forty-two, I was diagnosed with retinitis pigmentosa and told I would need a white cane or a guide dog in the not-too-distant future. Since I was on my way to participate in my weekly poker game at the Temple University faculty club in Philadelphia, this prediction caught me totally off-guard. Unable to comprehend this news, I went on to participate in the poker game and had my biggest winning night ever!

I had recently left the faculty at Temple University to accept a position as professor of anthropology at Baruch College in New York City. Having decided to continue residing in Philadelphia, my travels between these two cities involved a complicated commute. While still trying to use my limited residual vision, I had two terrifying experiences in which I fell off the subway platform onto the tracks.

As the ophthalmologist predicted, my sight continued to deteriorate and I learned to use a white cane. In the academic year 1980–1981, I took a sabbatical, got a research grant and went to India to do anthropological fieldwork. In Indian cities, sidewalks are rare and pedestrians share the roadway with bicycles, bicycle-driven rickshaws, bullock carts, cows, cars and buses. Under these conditions, my white cane lost much of its effectiveness as a mobility aid. I felt compelled to rely on sighted guides as my safest and most effective mobility tools.

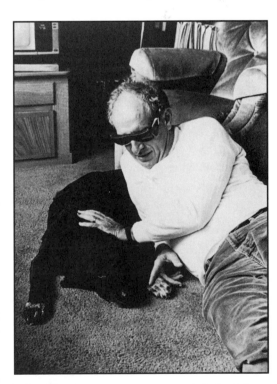

I never owned a pet and did not consider myself a dog lover. My wife was even less enthusiastic about dogs but recognized my need for a safer and more effective mobility aid. In the course of rehabilitation I had met several guide dog

Ed and Perrier.   Avigdar Adams

partners and was impressed with their confidence and ability to get around. So when I returned to the states, the first thing I did was apply for a guide dog.

In August 1981, I spent a month at The Seeing Eye™ in Morristown, New Jersey training with my black Labrador Retriever, Perrier. I thought I was simply going to get a more effective mobility aid and had no inkling of the impact this dog would have on my life.

Three days after my return home, Perrier and I set off on our commute from Philadelphia to New York. Following the same route I had used for years, I was amazed at the ease with which Perrier guided me on and off trains, subways and buses. He handled the streets of New York as if born for the task. My colleagues at Baruch welcomed Perrier and students seemed more relaxed about my blindness with a dog in the classroom. I'm not sure how much anthropology Perrier learned from attending my classes since he snored his way through most of them. On the other hand, I have the same question about most of my students, who at least had the good manners not to snore!

My increased feelings of independence and self-reliance became a sore point with my wife. Although she did not mind my need to care for Perrier—feeding, providing water, daily outings for relief and occasional visits to the veterinarian—she did resent the attention Perrier drew when he accompanied us to restaurants, theaters, religious services and the homes of friends. She saw no need for Perrier's presence when she could assume the guiding role. On the other hand, my children and grandchildren readily incorporated him as a member of the family.

Professors are always seeking new areas of interest for research and publication and I was no exception. As my relationship with Perrier blossomed, I became intrigued with the guide dog/blind person partnership. Questions began churning around in my mind. Why do some people opt for partnership with guide dogs? On what basis do people select particular training programs? Does having a guide dog help or hinder employment prospects? How do training programs select canine and student applicants? What are the advantages and disadvantages of working with a guide dog?

Obviously, these burning issues required immediate research and could only be adequately addressed in a book! My research brought me face-to-face with a variety of blindness-related issues that pushed me toward the assumption of an advocacy role. My wife, who was a very private person, became increasingly uncomfortable with my outspoken advocacy. Ultimately, our marriage ended in divorce.

After my divorce and subsequent marriage to Toni, I discovered it was fun living and traveling with two dogs. Although I had never considered myself an animal person, I had no difficulty becoming part of a family consisting of dogs and cats. After our move to California, we became itinerant educators and writers.

Unfortunately, Perrier had to be euthanized two years after our move. My feeling that he was magic and irreplaceable is shared by many of those who have lost their first partners in independence. The transition to a successor dog is usually emotionally wrenching. When I began working with Kirby at Guide Dogs of the Desert in Palm Springs, California, I compared him unfavorably with Perrier. Where Perrier's guiding style was confident, Kirby's was cautious. However, Kirby was far more outgoing and his exuberance and joy of life soon endeared this lovable Golden Retriever to me and all who met him.

Although Kirby's short working life was spent in Fresno, he was equally at ease in our travels to New York, San Francisco, Philadelphia and Boston. Like Ivy, he earned an AKC Companion Dog Excellent title. However, his major claim to fame occurred after the amputation of his left front leg as a result of bone cancer. His rehabilitation and resumption of work as my guide was an historic event. Everyone who saw his un-Golden-like tail continuously waving over his back realized this enthusiastic dog took pride in his work.

Grief at the loss of Kirby exceeded the feelings I had when Perrier was euthanized. At least Perrier had a full working life of eight years, while Kirby was euthanized after only four-and-a-half years of our partnership. At the end of July, 1994, I went to Leader Dogs to train with Jake, a twenty-one-month-old Golden. This match did not work and after eight months of concerted effort I had to admit defeat. Jake is now living a very happy life as a pet and companion in the home of a friend.

Still reeling from the dual effect of Kirby's death and Jake's inability to succeed as a guide, I found it difficult to bond with Echo, my new Golden guide from Leader Dogs. Echo came into my life just before his second and my sixty-fifth birthday. In contrast to Escort's exuberance, Echo's in-home style is more mellow. Although the bonding process took a long time in this match, he is now truly my friend and working partner.

History of the Assistance Dog Movement

The pioneering guide dog school in the United States, The Seeing Eye™, was established in 1929. It was inspired by earlier work with blind veterans in Germany during and after the First World War. Buddy, a German Shepherd Dog, and her blind partner, Morris Frank, a founder of The Seeing Eye™, trained in Switzerland and came back to the United States where Morris publicized the advantages of working with a guide dog.

Dorothy Harrison Eustis, a wealthy American living in Switzerland, had observed blind German veterans being guided by trained dogs. She wrote an article for the *Saturday Evening Post* describing what she had seen and offering to work with an interested blind American at her Fortunate Fields Kennels in Switzerland. Of the hundreds of responses she received, Dorothy chose the 19-year-old Morris because he expressed an intense desire for independence and the drive to achieve his goal of establishing an American guide dog training program. When Morris returned to the United States, the press jumped on this new concept of a dog who could be relied on to safely guide a blind person as the team negotiated heavy traffic, throngs of people and a diverse assortment of dangerous obstacles. Despite positive media coverage, when Morris approached several well-known organizations for the blind for support, his dream of developing a guide dog training program in the United States was summarily dismissed. Fulfilling Dorothy's faith in him, Morris persevered and attracted the needed public support to convert their dream into reality.

Blind person/guide dog partnerships proved to be so successful that within ten years another school was established. Then, as a result of the Second World War, several new programs were created to serve blind veterans. The majority of the fourteen guide dog schools operating in the United States today were, in fact, founded after World War II.

Initially, the German Shepherd Dog was the breed of choice for guide dog work. However, the majority of trained guides today are Labrador Retrievers, with German Shepherd Dogs and Golden Retrievers constituting most of the balance. Among other breeds in service to blind people are Doberman Pinschers, Boxers, Collies, Australian Shepherds and Standard Poodles. Guide dog candidates primarily come from breeding programs established by the various schools. Some schools, particularly the smaller and less affluent, accept donated puppies and dogs.

Each year approximately 1,300 blind person/guide dog teams graduate from the fourteen United States schools. Approximately half are seeking partnership with dogs for the first time, and the remainder are training with successor dogs. It is estimated that 7,500 teams are currently working in this country. With an estimated population of 1,100,000 legally blind Americans, this constitutes a very small portion of those who could benefit from such partnerships.

In contrast to the more than sixty-five years of blind Americans being partnered with guide dogs, deaf, hearing-impaired and physically disabled Americans have had only twenty years of experience working with hearing and service dogs. Interestingly, these two innovative approaches to the training and use of dogs do not seem to have influenced each other.

Bonita Bergin is the pioneer in the service dog movement. Having observed donkeys and other animals

In 1928 Morris Frank trained with Buddy in Switzerland. After returning to the United States, the team launched the guide dog movement in this country. Courtesy of The Seeing Eye™

assisting people with physical disabilities in several underdeveloped countries, she conceived the idea of harnessing the energy and intelligence of dogs to work with mobility impaired individuals. When she sought advice from guide dog training programs, they were not responsive and offered little help in transforming her idea into reality. Paralleling the determination and single-mindedness of Morris

Frank, she persevered and developed the first service dog training program in the country, Canine Companions for Independence, in Santa Rosa, California. As public awareness of the value of dogs serving people with disabilities was sparked by extensive media coverage, the demand for trained service dogs exploded, and many new training programs were established to meet the need.

As with guide dogs, Golden and Labrador Retrievers and German Shepherd Dogs are most often recruited for this work. With program waiting lists ranging from two to five years, many disabled people have chosen to train their own dogs or hire obedience trainers to prepare their pet dogs for service work. As a result, a large number of breeds can be seen assisting people with physical disabilities. Service dog candidates are generally donated to or rescued from shelters by the programs, although a small number of schools breed their own candidates.

While Bonita Bergin was initiating the service dog movement in the mid-seventies, Agnes McGrath was independently establishing a program to train dogs to assist people who were deaf or hard of hearing. The first training school began operation at the Minnesota Society for the Prevention of Cruelty to Animals and within a year was taken over by the American Humane Association (AHA) in Colorado. Unlike The Seeing Eye™ and Canine Companions for Independence, the AHA hearing dog program did not survive. However, it gave rise to a number of hearing dog training programs that can be seen as direct descendants of Agnes' original efforts.

In contrast to guide dog programs that have stressed the need for breeding suitable canine recruits, the hearing dog movement, with few exceptions, has remained committed to the founders' mission of rescuing suitable candidates from shelters and humane societies. As a result, hearing dogs come in all sizes and breed mixes.

More than fifty programs prepare dogs for working with people with disabilities other than blindness. There are two major factors making it impossible to obtain accurate statistics for the number of teams trained each year and the number of working teams. First, many training programs do not belong to Assistance Dogs International (ADI), a coalition of guide, hearing and service dog organizations. Second, many dogs are privately trained, making an accurate census impossible. Our best estimate is that 4,000 hearing dog teams and 3,500 service dog teams exist. Combining the figures for guide, hearing and service dogs, a total of 15,000 assistance dogs are currently working in the United States.

The Importance of Language

Words can empower, encourage, confuse, denigrate, delight or depress. George Orwell, in his book, *1984,* illustrated the political power of words. Some Orwellian disciples continue to track the way words are used to modify the impact of reality.

Following the lead of feminists and African-Americans, disabled people have recognized the power of language in reshaping societal attitudes and images. Terms such as cripple, invalid, wheelchair-bound and deaf and dumb are no longer acceptable. With the signing of the Americans with Disabilities Act (ADA), a law guaranteeing civil rights for an estimated 49 million disabled Americans, the politically correct term for those of us who are blind, deaf or mobility impaired is "disabled." Handicaps are the barriers placed in the path of disabled people preventing them from full participation in society. Thus, blindness is our disability. One of our handicaps is not being able to read a print newspaper. However, with use of modern technology, even this handicap can be minimized. Restaurants that do not provide braille menus and hotels that do not provide tactile or braille numbers on rooms impose barriers to the independence of the disabled. These are examples of societally induced handicaps.

Because ADI is the industry-wide coalition of training programs, it has adopted "assistance dog" as the inclusive term for guide, hearing and service dogs.

"Guide dog" is the preferred generic term for a dog who guides a blind or visually impaired person. "Dog guide" is used by some but, as far as we are concerned, to parallel other dog activities such as sled dog, herding dog, guard dog, lap dog, etc. the function of the dog should come first. To us a dog guide is a book about dogs and a dog service has funereal overtones. The title Seeing Eye™, belonging to the first guide dog school in this country, is a registered trademark. Most Americans use the term seeing eye interchangeably with the generic term guide dog. However, it should only be used for dogs graduated from the school in Morristown, New Jersey. The public's confusion and incorrect usage is reinforced by members of the mass media who incorrectly continue to use seeing eye as an equivalent term for guide dog, without regard to where the dog received training.

The preferred term for dogs assisting deaf or hard of hearing people is "hearing dog." When Canine Companions for Independence began training these dogs, they referred to them as signal dogs. Although personally we prefer this term since it is more descriptive of what these dogs do, the industry eventually settled on hearing dog as the generic term.

While "service dog" is the term preferred by ADI for dogs assisting people with physical disabilities, a variety of other terms is being used for these working dogs. Occasionally, they are referred to by their functions, such as support, wheelchair pulling or seizure alert dogs.

Unfortunately, in its attempt to guarantee access for disabled people partnered with dogs who assist them, the writers of the guidelines for the ADA confused the language issue by using the term "service" rather than "assistance animals." The broader term animals was chosen to protect the rights of disabled people partnered with Capuchin monkeys. However, the use of the word service was, in our opinion, not well thought out. Service dog, as noted above, is the term used to describe a dog who assists an individual with a mobility impairment. A further source of confusion for the public is the use of service dog for working military and police dogs. Once again, language confuses rather than clarifies.

A term used throughout the assistance dog industry, anathema to us, is "replacement dog." When a beloved and trusted assistance dog retires or dies, we may seek a new partnership. Although the new dog will replace the assistive functions we valued in our previous canine assistant, no dog ever replaces a beloved partner. Each dog is unique and has a special place in our hearts and lives. When programs suggest returning for a replacement dog, they devalue and diminish the relationship with the former canine partner. We have suggested to the industry the more humane term "successor dog." However, like most linguistic changes, it will take a long time before this usage becomes widely accepted.

Linguistic controversy does not end with dog terminology; it spills over onto the human end of the leash. Are we masters, owners, users or handlers? Personally, we prefer the term "partners."

Each term has its adherents and detractors. Although some of the assistance dog program literature refers to us as masters, this term is no longer in favor in the general dog training community. The term handler currently in vogue implies dominance without enslavement. However, many disabled people see themselves as assistance dog users, reserving the term handlers for the professionals who trained their dogs. We don't like user because, like master, it smacks of exploitation. Owner is inappropriate because many assistance dog programs retain title to our dogs. Partner seems to us to be a humane and descriptive term, but even this term is discounted by some on the grounds that it implies equality between human and dog.

Not only is there confusion about the term describing the relationship between disabled people and their canine helpers, but there is also considerable disagreement about what to call us when we apply for and train with our dogs. What should we be called after training is completed? We would like to be considered consumers, but most providers refer to us as clients. The term we find most objectionable is "recipient." This term is frequently used by the mass media to describe those who are needy and receive societal largesse. To us, recipient implies a paternalistic gift and de-emphasizes our effort to ensure an effective working partnership with our dogs. As recipients, we are expected to remain beholden to our training programs. Rather than projecting the image of the receipt of the trained dog as a gift, we would like to see language used emphasizing the participatory nature of our end of the relationship. A favorable term used in the industry, "participant" acknowledges us as more than recipients. Unlike recipient, participant does not symbolize a power imbalance.

Since training programs teach individuals to work with assistance dogs, we would like to see the industry adopt language used in the educational sector. Following the educational model, we would prefer the terms "applicant," "student" and "graduate."

Just as dogs need clear and consistent use of language to learn and respond to humans, humans need clear and consistent use of language to understand and respond to one another. Our goal in raising the issue of language has been to educate the general public about the correct terminology for guide, hearing and service dogs and to offer suggestions to the assistance dog industry to make it more responsive to its disabled constituency.

Chapter Two

Our Travels with Guide Dogs

Working with canine assistants increases independence for people with disabilities. A significant element in independent living is the ability to travel without the assistance of another person. Whether travel means going to the neighborhood store, visiting friends and relatives, commuting to work or touring foreign countries, the capacity to go from point A to point B with ease, comfort and safety is a central theme in the lives of many disabled people. For approximately 15,000 disabled Americans, the solution to their mobility and travel concerns has been partnership with guide, hearing and service dogs.

Coast to Coast

After our wedding in June 1987, we planned to spend Ed's sabbatical year in California. As born and raised eastern urbanites, our fantasy was to live in a small, uncongested city. San Francisco had the promise of convenient mass transportation; Los Angeles had the glamour of Hollywood; coastal cities, such as San Diego and Santa Barbara, had the lure of delightful weather. However, we chose Fresno, not known for good weather, good transportation or glamour, because Ed was able to obtain a visiting professorship at the California State University branch in Fresno and we could conduct research on attitudes toward blindness in this ethnically diverse community.

In many ways, Fresno is the antithesis of New York City. People are friendly, helpful and polite. Friends offered to find an apartment for us, but we declined their offers. For us, selecting a new home was like buying a pair of new shoes; only we would know when the fit was comfortable.

We flew to Fresno late in the summer of 1987 to find an apartment close to public transportation and within walking distance of a food market. "No pets" policies do not apply to our guide dogs. However, these exclusionary policies did apply to our cats, Disney and Tevye. As a result, we had to exclude two-thirds of the available Fresno rentals. At the end of a frantic four-day search, during which a relay of sighted friends chauffeured us around, we found a townhouse that was perfect for us.

Back in New York, we dealt with the myriad of details involved in a cross-country move. Of all these details, the most crucial was transporting the cats. Ivy and Perrier travel in the passenger cabin and curl up under the seats in front of us. Some airlines allow small pets to accompany their owners on board if the pet fits in a small crate placed under the seat in front of the passenger. Unfortunately for Tevye and Disney, this space was preempted by Perrier and Ivy. A very special woman, Mary Strain, manager of American Airlines Special Services at John F. Kennedy International Airport, rescued us from our dilemma by providing extra seats so each animal had his/her own space.

Sweet-natured Tevye became frantic when enclosed in a carrying case. His pitiful yowls could curl the hair of even the most committed cat lover. Surprisingly, high-strung Disney traveled quietly in a carrying case. On the advice of our veterinarian, we sedated both cats to save our fellow passengers from six hours of loud and pathetic meowing.

On the day of our flight, we did not know who was more nervous, the cats or us. Ivy and Perrier, accustomed to flying, were probably the calmest members of the family. Our tensions were partially relieved by an unusual occurrence—a New York City taxi driver who was friendly, helpful and polite. Two lovely women from American Airlines Special Services Department met us at Kennedy Airport. When they noticed how heavy the cat carriers were, they commandeered a wheelchair and placed both cases in it. Our entourage must have startled many blasé air travelers—two cats in a wheelchair being pushed by two American Airlines employees followed by two dogs guiding two blind people.

The California lifestyle suited the six of us so well we decided to extend our sabbatical into a permanent living arrangement. Unfortunately, shortly after our move, Tevye developed the unacceptable habit of spraying in the house. We tried every medical and behavioral solution, but could not solve this problem. Further complicating our lives was the deterioration of Perrier's health. With great regret and sadness, we had both of our beloved friends and companions euthanized in October 1989.

Despite our continuing love affair with Fresno, several unanticipated problems emerged which have had a negative impact on local travel. Unlike New York City, where a blade of grass is a rarity, in Fresno every lawn and yard boasts a profusion of lush trees, bushes and shrubs. Much of this foliage protrudes into the walkway. One of the most difficult obstacle-avoidance behaviors for a guide dog to master is overhanging branches above the dog's eye level. When we first moved here, Ed was thrilled when he was hit in the head with an orange hanging from a neighbor's tree. It is no longer amusing. To remedy the situation, once every couple of weeks, Ed takes our pruning shears and helps our negligent neighbors with their gardening chores!

In New York, subway and bus transportation is available around the clock. In contrast, Fresno buses run from 6 A.M. to 7 P.M. Since bus drivers usually announce stops, our problems begin when we get off the bus. In an unfamiliar area we are likely to encounter railroad tracks, irrigation canals and areas with no sidewalks. As rare as a blade of grass is in New York City, a pedestrian is equally rare in Fresno. Since we cannot depend upon getting directional information from a kind passerby, we often scout out a new route with a sighted friend before venturing out on our own. In rare situations, when we have gotten confused or lost and no one has come along to advise us, Ed has hailed a passing motorist to help reorient us.

In walking along the streets of Philadelphia, New York City or San Francisco, we use the building line for orientation. Unfortunately, in Fresno most business establishments are fronted by huge, open parking lots. To work effectively, guide dogs need clear directional commands. We cannot give these commands unless we know our exact location. When we tell the dogs Right and Inside, it is difficult for them to obey when the nearest building is 500 yards away! A solution for us is to phone ahead and ask the storekeeper, restaurant manager or business proprietor to watch for us and meet us at curbside. Once the dogs have learned a particular route, they can repeat it without assistance.

Visiting New York

After a whirlwind trip in the summer of 1992 to Kansas, Michigan, Canada and Florida during which we visited five guide dog schools in eleven days, we looked forward to a bit of rest and relaxation in New York. This respite would provide the opportunity to visit friends and relatives, give Ed the chance to swim in the Atlantic Ocean and allow us to visit a sixth guide dog school, Guide Dog Foundation in Smithtown, located in Long Island's Suffolk County.

Kirby, Perrier's successor, had been raised and trained in southern California and had never been exposed to the hustle and bustle of a city like New York. With a week of planned activities ahead of us, we wondered how he would cope with subway travel, crowded streets and the noise of sirens, beeping horns and screeching brakes. For Ivy, visiting New York would be a return to a familiar environment.

Kirby met the challenge of his first trip into Manhattan with aplomb. We traveled on the Long Island Rail Road from our friend Eleanor Marugo's home in Huntington, traversed the crowds in Penn Station, took a taxi to the Broadway discount ticket booth and, after purchasing tickets, conquered the Broadway mob scene to meet Toni's cousin Edward Hendel for lunch. A subsequent visit to Manhattan several days later to see another Broadway play also gave us the opportunity to have lunch with Stef and David Wilner, Toni's aunt and uncle.

Kirby got his first subway ride when we traveled from Manhattan to Coney Island to stay with our friend, Paulette Nossen and her eleven-year-old black Labrador guide dog Laina. That evening we were joined for dinner by another blind friend, Bob Feinstein, with his eleven-year old yellow Labrador guide Flynn.

Earlier in the week, Ed had indulged his passion for playing in the waves, but couldn't pass up the opportunity to dip into the Atlantic just one more time. You may be wondering why, as a Californian, Ed has this passion for swimming in the Atlantic. Despite the Hollywood depiction of California as a land of sun bathers and swimmers, most of the state's coastline borders on water that is too cold, rocky and rough for swimmers. Although Coney Island is better known for its amusement parks and hot dogs than for its beach,

Ed was lured by the memory of lapping waves, seventy degree water temperature and soft sand.

In contrast to our previous swimming excursions, Ed would have no sighted friends to guide him. We didn't let that fact get in our way. A passion is a passion! We had a strategy and it worked. Paulette accompanied us to the boardwalk where Ivy found a bench. Ed asked a passerby to walk him down to the water's edge and introduce him to the lifeguard. The lifeguard said she would watch for Ed when he emerged from the water and walk back with him to the boardwalk where Paulette and Toni waited with the three dogs. Swimming in the ocean as a blind person is not a problem since the noise of the crowd and the motion of the waves provide orientation. Ed thoroughly enjoyed his adventure, while Toni, a fuddy-duddy about sand and salt water, enjoyed her visit with Paulette on dry land.

Most of our time in New York was spent with Eleanor in Huntington, Long Island. Toni and Eleanor had been co-workers at Kings Park Psychiatric Center (KPPC) and we had the opportunity to visit with many former colleagues. Since Eleanor's property is secured by a fenced-in yard, we let the dogs romp around in back. All that ended when we heard the next door neighbors commenting about two Golden Retrievers playing in their yard. We pondered the fickleness of the canine mind as we were in the process of training Ivy and Kirby for American Kennel Club Open competition and they sometimes approached the high jump as if it were an insurmountable obstacle. Yet, a four-foot fence was no barrier to their desire to explore the neighbors' yard!

One evening we had dinner with Toni's sister Lorraine Sosne. Lorraine, like Toni, is a dog lover and shares her home with two Cavalier King Charles Spaniels and a Bichon Frise. To Lorraine's surprise, we requested pizza for dinner. Eating California's version of pizza for the last five years has left us with a craving for the real thing. With fond memories of New York pizza, we drooled in anticipation of this well-remembered culinary delight. When the pizza was delivered, the smell was right, the texture was right, but the taste was pure California!

Moving away from New York meant not only giving up outstanding ethnic food, but, more importantly, leaving behind well-loved friends and family. One such friend we were delighted to spend time with was Jerry Tobias. In 1967 Jerry became the veterinarian for Toni's animals. In 1983 their friendship was cemented when Flicka, Ivy's predecessor, was being treated for lymphosarcoma. After Ed came into Toni's life, Jerry assumed the care of Perrier, Kirby's predecessor. When we were planning our wedding, Jerry generously offered his home for the ceremony and reception. Despite our move to California, he has remained closely involved with the health of our animal family. A year after our wedding, Jerry met and married Alice, a warm and wonderful woman. The rainstorm that raged outside did not dampen the delightful evening we spent with the Tobiases.

Another former colleague we got to see was Dorothy Dengel. Although Toni and Dorothy worked in the same building at KPPC, they did not become good friends until the death of Dorothy's pet dog in the late 1970s. Because of her housing circumstances, she was unable to get another dog. Needing canine companionship, Dorothy suggested playing ball with Flicka during her coffee breaks.

Those who are familiar with Golden Retrievers know they have a tennis ball gene, and Toni jumped at the chance of letting her city-dwelling dog enjoy chasing tennis balls in an open area. Dorothy was so devoted to these romps, she never let rain or snow get in the way of playtime. When Flicka heard Dorothy approaching Toni's office, she gathered three tennis balls in her mouth and was raring to go.

After Flicka's death, Ivy inherited this passion for playtime with Dorothy. Although Ivy had not seen her for three years, as soon as she spotted Dorothy waiting for us on the subway platform, she began trembling with anticipation. Kirby, who had never met Dorothy, picked up Ivy's excitement and greeted Dorothy like a long-lost friend. For the next two days, Ivy and Kirby must have thought they were in tennis ball heaven.

Pursuing Our New Career

On April 19, 1994, we took off on a 15-day cross-country trip sponsored by American Airlines. The purpose of the trip was to educate veterinarians about assistance dogs and to advocate on behalf of disabled people partnered with guide, hearing and service dogs.

Our first stop was Kansas City, where our friend Diane Anderson met us at the airport. We drove into the city to have dinner with Cindy Robin and Bill Stephan and their guide dogs, a Siberian Husky and a Border Collie. The next morning, Diane drove us to the Kansas City Zoo where we had a pre-arranged tour. Following the tour we had a wonderful lunch in a famous Kansas City barbecue restaurant. We then drove with Diane three-and-a-half hours to north central Kansas to visit a friend getting a guide dog at Kansas Specialty Dog Service (KSDS). Since this was our fourth trip to KSDS, we enjoyed visiting with old friends. It was fun getting acquainted with the students in training, their families and new canine partners.

The next stop on our itinerary was Philadelphia, where we were scheduled to speak to the veterinary students at the University of Pennsylvania. It was invigorating to be back in a major urban setting with lots of people on the street. Therefore, we decided to walk from our hotel to the veterinary school. As we approached our destination, Ed asked a passerby to direct us to the vet hospital. We were disconcerted upon entering a crowded lobby bereft of the sounds of barking dogs and meowing cats. Sure enough, our helpful passerby had inadvertently directed us to the Veterans Administration Hospital! Fortunately, the veterinary hospital was directly across the street. Despite this comedy of errors, we arrived at our lecture on time.

Some people enjoy seeing the sights unique to a city when they travel; Ed enjoys eating the foods unique to a city we visit. With only one night in Philadelphia, a city he had lived in for more than thirty years, Ed indulged in a cheese steak, a hoagie and a pretzel!

The next stop on our tour was Morristown, New Jersey, where we visited The Seeing Eye™, Perrier's alma mater. After a tour of the facility followed by a fabulous lunch, we chatted with members of the staff about changes taking place at the school. One of the more spectacular changes has been the expansion of staff, dormitory and kennel facilities to accommodate a thirty-percent increase in the number of teams graduated annually.

Whenever we travel, we try to combine work with pleasure. We spent that evening with friends, Melanie and Allen Whitesides, in New Jersey, one of many pleasurable interludes between our lecturing and advocacy activities. Melanie and Toni were co-workers at KPPC, and Allen was one of the singers at our wedding.

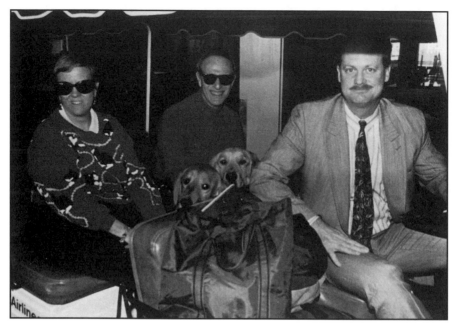

Toni and Escort and Ed and Echo receive VIP treatment from American Airlines Special Service Department at Dallas–Fort Worth airport.   Courtesy of American Airlines

During our stay in New York, we attended the Broadway production of *Miss Saigon* and enjoyed the company of friends and relatives. We also attended an open-house farewell party at Kennedy Airport for Mary Strain, who was retiring as manager of American Airlines Special Services. Mary was instrumental in obtaining the travel grant for our trip and helped arrange our initial move to Fresno. Everyone was delighted to meet the dogs since a feature article about them had just appeared in the American Airlines JFK newsletter.

Another exciting part of our trip was meeting one of our heroes, Roger Caras, president of the American Society for the Prevention of Cruelty to Animals (ASPCA). His coverage of animal issues while working for national television did much to promote respect for domestic and wild animals. We were pleased to meet Roger before our presentation to the ASPCA veterinary staff at the Bergh Memorial Hospital.

The last leg of our trip was spent in Boston. Once again, we combined visits with friends and family with our educational mission. On May 2, we spoke to the staff of the Angell Memorial Hospital, the medical arm of the Massachusetts SPCA. After our talk we were given a tour of this impressive state-of-the-art animal hospital. Although this facility serves many thousands of animals each year, the staff seems to have retained its compassion for human clients as well as animal patients. Dr. Paul Gambardella, hospital administrator, told us about a German Shepherd guide dog who recently underwent hip replacement surgery. This six-year-old dog had severe arthritis in one hip. Immediately after the surgical procedure, the dog was unwilling to put weight on the new hip and was content to function on three legs. Various techniques to get him to again be four-legged were being tried. With Kirby's success as a three-legged dog after amputation of his leg, we knew how easily a dog could adapt to three-leggedness.

Tuesday evening's presentation to the veterinary students at Tufts University was preceded by a pizza party. Dr. Frank Loew, Dean of the veterinary school, told us about the close relationship between Tufts and Fidelco Guide Dog Foundation and New England Assistance Dog Service. The enthusiasm of this group of students reinforced the significance of our mission and spurred us on to take our message to all twenty-seven veterinary schools.

A trip to the East Coast without access problems would be highly unusual. We were not to be disappointed! On two occasions in New York and one in Boston, taxi drivers had to be convinced they would be breaking the law if they continued to refuse to allow us to ride with our dogs.

Bermuda

In 1990 our friend Anne Glaser suggested contacting Betty Leighton, president of the World Congress of Kennel Clubs, about speaking to the Congress during its meeting in Bermuda in November 1992. Anne, a prominent obedience instructor, met Toni in New York in the early 1970s when Toni was participating with Charm in AKC Obedience competition. In the mid-1980s when Ed was having a problem with Perrier, Anne came to his rescue and offered suggestions that helped resolve the problem. Like us, Anne subsequently abandoned the East Coast and moved west with her husband and dogs.

Following Anne's advice, we wrote to Betty. To our great joy and delight, she responded favorably to our offer and presented us with a formal invitation to speak to the Congress. The topics we chose were: blind handlers in the Obedience ring, the assistance dog movement in the United States and grief at the loss of a guide dog through retirement or death. Betty also invited us to participate in the five days of dog shows preceding the World Congress.

Knowing Bermuda is a British colony, we were intrigued to learn there were no quarantine restrictions preventing us from entering the country with our Goldens. Bermuda, a rabies-free country, requires documentation of rabies and parvo inoculations and proof that a flea and tick bath has been given to the dog within ten days of entry. As Bermudians quip, "We don't want American ticks and fleas, but you are welcome to leave with ours!"

Betty asked Elfreda Lines, a member of the Bermuda Dog Training Club, to coordinate our stay. For the six months before our trip, we carried on a lively correspondence with Elfreda. She sent us tourist brochures and the Bermuda Kennel Club Obedience rule book. In her letters to us, Elfreda mentioned Jean Howes, the only guide dog partner in Bermuda. Before our trip, we contacted Jean to inquire about guide dog access to public places. Jean was excited about the prospect of our visit, but warned us about the lack of legal access rights. However, she told us most Bermudians are dog lovers and predicted we were unlikely to meet with discrimination.

Although November 1992 seemed so remote when we first spoke with Anne, before we knew it we found ourselves on a flight heading for Bermuda. Elfreda and another club member, Ann Sousa, met us at the airport and drove us to our hotel. Like the British, Bermudians drive on the left side of the road, but, unlike the British who drive at breakneck speeds, Bermudians have a twenty-two mph speed limit. We settled into our mini-suite at the Royal Palms, a small hotel on the outskirts of the city of Hamilton.

On the afternoon of our arrival, we planned to take the opportunity to catch up on lost sleep because we had been traveling since 7 P.M. the previous night. However, we were so delighted to finally meet Elfreda that we spent several hours chatting and getting to know her better. Throughout our stay, we looked forward to Elfreda's evening visits when we talked dogs and caught up on the events of the day.

While visiting Bermuda, Ed and Toni experience the punishment meted out to miscreants during colonial times. While Lion member Margaret Vaucrosson looks on, Ivy and Kirby enjoy a break from guide work.

With Elfreda's help, we had developed a work- and fun-filled itinerary. At Jean Howes' suggestion, one of the people we contacted in advance of our trip was Margaret Vaucrosson, a member of the Hamilton Lioness Club. Margaret was delighted to accept our offer to speak to her club and asked if the Lions and Lioness Clubs could assist us in any way. We told her of our need for escorts to tourist attractions and to and from the dog show grounds. Margaret organized and coordinated a corps of volunteers to meet our escort needs.

Our first five mornings in Bermuda were taken up with dog shows. Afternoons were set aside for sightseeing and socializing. Accompanied by members of the Lions and Lioness Clubs, we explored a living cave, strolled on the beach, took a ferry ride to a craft fair, toured a perfumery and enjoyed the ocean breezes and narration on a glass-bottom boat trip to the nearby coral reef.

Margaret and her husband Charles took us to historic St. George's, the site of the 1609 settlement of Bermuda. Bonding with this warm, charming and dynamic couple was unavoidable. Charles took time from his busy law practice not only to drive us from our hotel to the show grounds each morning, but also to chauffeur us around to other events. We couldn't have asked for a more knowledgeable and prominent guide. In fact, the only people who didn't know Charles were first-time visitors to the island!

Of course, Ivy and Kirby were an integral part of these excursions. Despite the lack of laws guaranteeing assistance dog access, our Goldens were welcome everywhere we went. Jean Howes' assessment of Bermudians as dog lovers was confirmed.

One of the first days, Jean invited us to her home for lunch. Although we could have arranged for a ride, on this occasion we preferred taking public transportation. Jean was excited by the thought of three guide dogs on the bus, an historic event in Bermuda. Whether on the street or in the bus, everyone seemed to know and greet Jean and her yellow Labrador Mandy.

We met Jean several times during our stay. She was a co-speaker at the Lioness Club dinner held at the Dinghy Club. We hold the Lions and Lioness Clubs in high esteem for the work they do on behalf of blind people. One of their projects is providing support for all of the guide dog programs in the United States.

We were scheduled to depart from Bermuda on a 7 A.M. flight. This necessitated waking up by 4:30 A.M. Responding to our fear that the clock radio in our hotel room might not go off as planned, Elfreda and the Dog Training Club came to our rescue by purchasing an old-fashioned alarm clock to replace the one we forgot to bring. Everything went off without a hitch and we arrived home in Fresno later that day exhausted, but exhilarated!

Israel

On a hot August evening in 1995, we tried to distract ourselves with a variety of chores until the anticipated arrival of our friend Evie Rote and her family. We hadn't seen Evie for years and were excited about her forthcoming visit to Fresno.

Our first meeting with Evie took place in 1986 when we traveled to Israel from our home in New York City to present a paper at the

International Mobility Conference. In contrast to our trips to the United Kingdom, where we are forced to travel dogless because of the quarantine, Ivy and Perrier could accompany us to Israel.

Very little was needed to prepare the dogs for the trip to Israel. Not wanting to change their diet for the two-week stay, we packed an ample supply of their food. Required health certificates were obtained and carried with our passports. It was our assumption that the dogs, as seasoned guides, would work as well on the streets of Tel Aviv and Jerusalem as they did on the streets of New York, Philadelphia and Montreal. This belief was subsequently verified by their behavior.

Our immediate concern was for the dogs' comfort during the twelve-hour nonstop flight. Perrier and Ivy received limited amounts of food and water for several hours before we left for the airport. Taught to relieve on command, they took advantage of their relief break before we entered the taxi. Arriving at the international departure terminal at Kennedy Airport two hours before the scheduled flight, we sat around until boarding time. Entering the cabin, the dogs guided us to our seats and settled down under the seats in front of us where our carry-on luggage would normally be stowed. Each time we got up to use the toilet, we felt guilty about the poor dogs. Our painstaking planning was almost sabotaged by a thoughtless dog-loving flight attendant. While Ed slept, she began feeding Perrier some rolls left over from passengers' dinner trays. Feeling Perrier move to take advantage of this unexpected opportunity, Ed woke and, after learning what was going on, was furious with the well-meaning attendant. The consequence of feeding a dog on a long flight with no place for him to relieve himself had never occurred to her!

When the plane landed in Tel Aviv, we were told we had to wait until all the other passengers got off before we could deplane. Back in the United States, we would not have complied with this discriminatory treatment. However, we were on foreign soil and felt vulnerable. When we finally got off, we gave the dogs the opportunity to relieve themselves in a corner of the airfield, and Ivy gratefully complied. Although Perrier had not relieved himself in over fifteen hours, he declined this opportunity and waited an additional three hours until we arrived at the Hebrew University Faculty Club in Jerusalem where he finally took advantage of a grassy area to take care of his physical needs.

For the next few days we met conference participants from all parts of the world. Our paper on the research behind the preparation of our book on guide dog schools was well received. During one of the sessions, a baby crawled over to greet Perrier and Ivy. Later, during the break, the baby's mother, Evie Rote, introduced herself. We felt an instant bond with this warm effervescent American married to an Israeli. At the end of the conference we were delighted to accept her invitation to visit her the following week in Haifa.

Before embarking on our Israeli adventure, we had written to several Israeli guide dog partners. From Jerusalem, we traveled by bus to Kibbutz Degainai to visit Moti Levy, who was partnered with a guide dog. Moti and his family spoke very little English, so our interactions were sometimes very amusing. They invited us to accompany them to the hot mineral springs at Tiberius. One of the attractions was a water slide, but they did not have the English words to describe it. After several moments of confusion, we instantly comprehended when they made the sound "wheeee!" In Tiberius, Ed relished the excitement of climbing the steps to the top of the slide and zooming down, while Toni stood on terra firma holding the dogs.

A memorable experience we shared with the Levys was our day at the Kinneret (Sea of Galilee). Moti warned us that this volcanic formation had many crevices and one could suddenly step from ankle-deep water into the depths. Toni, a nonswimmer, chose the security of the shore. True to her heritage, Golden Retriever Ivy was so passionate about swimming she forgot the meaning of the recall command when allowed in the water. Therefore, Toni was afraid Ivy would end up in Jordan if allowed to swim. Disloyal to his Labrador heritage, Perrier hated to swim, and Ed felt comfortable allowing him to romp off-leash while Ed enjoyed playing in the water. As Perrier happily sniffed along the shoreline, he suddenly stepped into a crevice with water over his head. Panicking, he spotted Ed, and jumped on his back for protection. The weight of his struggling dog pushed Ed underwater several times. Realizing he was in danger, Ed shoved Perrier away and swam to the outstretched arms of the shouting onlookers. Following Ed's example, Perrier found the safety of the shore. After everyone had a chance to calm down and dry off, Toni joked about the unimaginable newspaper headline proclaiming, "Guide Dog Drowns Blind Partner During Vacation in Israel!"

During our two weeks in Israel, we met several other guide dog partners. Until recently, Israeli blind men and women travelled to the United States for training at American guide dog schools. Not only was this a financial burden for some, but for non-English speakers, the language barrier complicated the training process. Today Israelis no longer have to leave the country to become partnered with guide dogs. Several years ago the Israel Guide Dog Center for the Blind was established.

Before leaving on our trip, we were warned by a sighted Israeli professor friend of Ed's we were likely to have access problems with hotels and taxis. Actually, we faced fewer problems in Israel than we normally faced in New York City. In Tel Aviv, we planned to stay at a small family-owned hotel recommended by an American friend. When we made the reservations, we explained we were blind and would be accompanied by our guide dogs. The proprietor spoke very little English, and we were not sure he understood. Our fears were unfounded. If anything, the family was so enthralled by the presence

Ed and Perrier, Toni and Ivy visit Haifa University in Israel.

of the dogs that they became a major distraction by hugging and calling to Perrier and Ivy whenever we walked through the lobby. Our only Israeli access problem occurred when the proprietor hailed a taxi for us. When the driver refused to take the dogs, the proprietor became enraged, and a heated argument in Hebrew ensued.

Accepting Evie's generous offer to stay with her and her family, we made Haifa the final stop on our trip. Evie was on vacation from her job as a teacher of blind and disabled preschoolers. A highlight of being in Haifa was swimming in the Mediterranean Sea. On this occasion we went into the water with Evie's daughters while she dog sat.

Talking with Evie when she arrived in Fresno brought back all these memories and stimulated our desire to return to Israel. For our current guides, Escort and Echo, it would be their first trip to a foreign country.

Chapter Three

People Who Make It Happen

The assistance dog movement is an exciting and creative endeavor. From the older established programs like The Seeing Eye™, CCI and Dogs for the Deaf, to the recently founded programs like Southeastern Guide Dogs and KSDS, one has the feeling of energy, commitment and professionalism.

Following the model of existing guide dog training schools, most hearing and service dog training programs are nonprofit organizations. They provide canine partners for disabled people at minimal or no cost. Thus, their existence is based on philanthropic contributions from the public.

Maintaining an existing program or developing a new one is a daunting task. The programs compete with all other charities for scarce dollars. In addition, they frequently compete with one another for dogs, puppy raisers, students and volunteers.

On July 22, 1991, we began a three-week cross-country trip sponsored by a grant from American Airlines to visit six guide dog schools, three to be featured in this chapter. Our first stop was KSDS.

Kansas Specialty Dog Service

"Unique" is the name of a female Boxer in training to become a guide dog. Unique is also an apt description for this recently established assistance dog training program.

KSDS is the only nonprofit program established with the support of state funds. It is also one of the few programs training both guide and service dogs. The Kansas Departments of Rehabilitation and Commerce provided a three-year grant to develop a program to train service dogs for physically disabled people, guide dogs for blind people and social dogs for people and institutions in need of specially trained therapeutic canine companions.

For eighteen years, Bill Acree, Executive Director, and his wife, Karen, managed an office supply business in Washington, Kansas, a town of 1,800 in the north-central part of the state. Over the years,

they expanded their operation to include a print shop and a Sears catalogue outlet. After founding KSDS, using his business acumen, Bill negotiated a number of contractual relationships that relieve disabled people of the financial burdens they currently face when partnered with assistance dogs. When KSDS was established, IAMS™ donated food for foster puppies, dogs in training and working dogs graduated from the program. In addition, IAMS™ purchased the identifying capes worn by puppies being socialized, harnesses for guide dogs and packs for service dogs. In 1994, this sponsorship was taken over by Hills Science Diet. Bill refers to this support program as "cradle to grave care."

Bill negotiated a relationship with the Kansas Veterinary Medical Association (KVMA) and the veterinary school at Kansas State University to remove the financial burden of routine and emergency veterinary costs. The KVMA has rec-

Kansas Specialty Dog Service instructor Karen Acree trains Unique for guide work.
Courtesy KSDS

ommended to member veterinarians that they provide care at no cost or low cost from puppyhood through old age. Veterinarians who participate in this program are honored with plaques presented by the KVMA auxiliary.

During our visit to KSDS, we were impressed with the enthusiasm of the entire staff. In their eagerness to learn more about guide dog training, Karen and the other trainers accompanied us on

A class of student and dog trainees at Kansas Specialty Dog Service practices obedience in the midst of a multitude of distractions.   Courtesy of KSDS

several demonstration walks. With our permission, they worked Ivy and Kirby to get a feel for working with experienced guide dogs.

In the course of many hours of intense discussions and interactions, Toni was delighted to share her lap with Eli and Whitney, the KSDS resident office cats. She has a hard time leaving our three feline kids behind when we travel and is always comforted when cuddling someone else's cats. The presence of cats at an assistance dog training facility is not unusual. However, most programs restrict them to the kennel area. This limits the dogs' interaction with cats and, consequently, many assistance dogs are not well-behaved in their presence. By having cats living in the training area rather than the kennel, KSDS avoids this potential problem.

We are always intrigued with the stories behind the pioneers in the assistance dog movement. Like most of their peers, the folks at KSDS have a deep sense of mission. However, combined with this dream is a recognition of the practical problems involved in establishing an enduring program.

The Acrees, and co-founder Sarah Holbert, did not dream about training assistance dogs until recently. Sarah and Karen were 4-H leaders in their respective counties for youngsters involved with dog training. As county leaders, the Acrees and Holberts knew each other, but their friendship was cemented when they took on the joint project of fostering puppies for Pilot Dogs of Columbus, Ohio. Their yellow Labradors, Boomer and Oz, graduated as guide dogs and are currently working in Ohio and West Virginia. Their next venture was raising Golden Retriever littermates for CCI. Unfortunately, none of the Kansas-raised CCI puppies graduated as service dogs.

The need for assistance dogs by disabled Midwesterners was documented and this determined threesome went on a campaign to obtain the necessary support for establishing a Kansas-based program. Following months of meetings and negotiations with state legislators, they received a grant permitting them to begin operations. The First National Bank of Washington sold a vacant restaurant at a substantial discount to KSDS, which was then converted into a wheelchair accessible office and training center. The city of Washington donated land and paid for the construction of a fifty-run dog kennel. The Golden and Labrador Retrievers, Boxers and German Shepherd Dogs in residence enjoy the comfort of a modern, well-designed facility. With all of the local and state support received, KSDS was able to open its doors on September 1, 1990.

Unfettered by the established traditions of older programs, KSDS is free to explore new trends in both guide and service dog training. KSDS does not plan to invest in a dormitory facility; students will stay in nearby motels. This is not unusual for service dog programs, but is highly innovative in the guide dog field. With the exception of Fidelco Guide Dog Foundation which trains students in their home environment, guide dog schools require residence in a dormitory setting with a variety of restrictive rules. At KSDS, trainees will be required to attend training sessions, but will be on their own during nonworking time.

Bill notes the problems faced by many assistance teams when they return home. To forestall these problems, KSDS will encourage family members to participate in the program and learn about the training and function of their family member's new partner. Since KSDS will initially serve disabled people from Kansas, Nebraska and Missouri, families can travel to Washington and spend a weekend or several days getting to know the new team.

Dorothy was not the only one who longed to return to Kansas. We can hardly wait to return and see this innovative program grow and mature.

Freedom Service Dogs

We are all familiar with the adage, "Love me, love my dog." Mike Roche fell in love with Oreo, Paulette Jo Burrous' Border Collie. P.J., as she prefers to be called, laughingly suggests Mike married her in order to keep Oreo in the family.

In June 1978, Mike was working as a paramedic and was ministering to a patient in the back of an ambulance when it was involved in an accident. Mike sustained a spinal cord injury, paralyzing him from the neck down. After several months of physical and vocational rehabilitation, he obtained employment as a computer programmer.

P.J., who grew up in Dayton, Ohio, got involved in obedience training as a teenager. She bred Collies and showed them in conformation and Obedience. P.J. became an obedience instructor and by the time she moved to Denver in 1984, her breed of choice was the Border Collie.

After Mike and P.J. began dating, Mike would dog sit for Oreo when the Border Collie could not accompany P.J. Oreo, who had been trained for AKC Obedience competition, enjoyed retrieving, so Mike and P.J. capitalized on this skill and trained him to pick up objects Mike had dropped and return them to Mike's hand. As P.J. recollects, lights went off for them. They had read about the exploits of service dogs and decided to train Oreo to pull Mike's wheelchair, turn light switches on and off, open doors, carry things and, since Mike has limited lung capacity, bark for alarm when he has breathing problems.

While visiting a local rehabilitation center, a staff member impressed with the Roches' training of Oreo asked P.J. and Mike to train a dog for a disabled man who lived alone. Knowing the waiting time for a service dog from already established organizations was more than two years, P.J. and Mike accepted the challenge. As other disabled people approached them, they saw the need for a formal training program. Freedom Service Dogs, Inc. (FSDI) was born as a result of this growing consumer demand. It was incorporated as a

Freedom Service Dogs Inc. co-founders, Mike and P.J. Roche, check out a potential service dog candidate at a local animal shelter.   Leah Ames

nonprofit organization in October 1987, seven months after the Roches were married.

With all the mass media coverage of service dogs, the Roches are amazed at the public's lack of recognition of assistance dogs. Returning home from a trip to California two years ago, they were denied entry to a Las Vegas casino. Not being familiar with Nevada law, they did not realize they could have insisted on Oreo's legal right to accompany them into the casino. As a result of this experience, they decided to compile all the state laws concerning guide, hearing and service dogs in a single volume titled *Legal Rights of Guide Dogs, Hearing Dogs and Service Dogs.* Abridged and unabridged versions of this book are available from FSDI.

Like all assistance dog organizations, FSDI continually faces the need to obtain sufficient funds to support its activities. Although Mike and P.J. work from their own home without salary, the $18,000 they were able to raise last year allowed them to train only three teams. To help in fundraising, two volunteers have recently joined them and they hope to increase their funds and funding sources.

When P.J. and Mike are searching for suitable canine candidates, they travel to shelters and rescue leagues as far as twenty-five miles from their home. Prospective recruits are between one and two years old, have some Golden or Labrador Retriever in their breeding and are extremely outgoing. Dogs who try to lick or make physical contact with them through the bars of the kennel will be taken to a quiet room for further testing. P.J. observes the selected dog's reaction to a leash and collar. Mike, seated in his wheelchair, calls the dog to him. To test the dog's response to an unfamiliar situation, Mike, who is bearded, wears a hat. Any dog refusing to approach Mike with beard, hat and wheelchair is immediately rejected.

An essential qualification for selection is extreme people orientation. Mike and P.J. test for this quality by allowing the unleashed dog to wander around the room. The dog who is more interested in sniffing than responding to their call is rejected. P.J. believes it is easier to control a high level of exuberance than to instill confidence in a timid or fearful dog.

Another test determines the dog's reaction to a leash correction. A dog who is devastated by the correction and does not recover eagerness to please is rejected. Since the Roches use food rewards in their training of service dogs, they are looking for a dog motivated by food. After a period of play, P.J. suddenly turns the dog on his/her back to test for submissiveness. She will then pinch the dog's pad to test for pain sensitivity. On occasion, a service dog's paw will be run over by a wheelchair, therefore, they cannot have an intolerance for pain. Finally, Mike throws a metal feed bowl on the floor to test for skittishness.

After passing the initial evaluation, selected dogs are taken to Doctors David and Sara Robinson for hip X rays and a thorough examination. Dogs with bad hips or in poor health are returned to the shelter; those cleared by the veterinarians are neutered. The Robinsons are among a growing number of veterinarians in the United States donating their services to assistance dog programs at reduced or no cost. These caring canine health providers have expanded their role in FSDI by joining the advisory board. Sara was nominated for the Delta Society's 1991 Veterinarian of the Year Award. (The Delta Society is an organization promoting the human/animal bond through research, education and training.)

Dogs in training live in the Roches' home where they are crate trained and good house manners are reinforced. Over the next six months, dogs receive formal training as future working partners for disabled people.

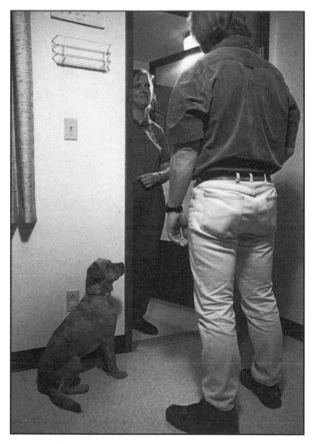

Hearing dog trainee Reno, a Labrador cross, is learning the door knock from Dogs for the Deaf trainer. Courtesy of DFD

Since its inception, FSDI has graduated fourteen teams at an average cost of $4,500 per team. Applicants must be over ten years old and must demonstrate willingness to take responsibility for the care of the dog. They initially demonstrate their interest by making a phone call to FSDI to initiate the application process.

Clients begin a three month training period after waiting approximately a year from the time of submitting completed applications. They train for three hours three times a week at a local mall and at the Roches' home. Trainees commute from their homes for these sessions and do not take their new partners home until they become proficient in handling their dog.

P.J. and Mike stay in close contact with their graduates. An annual recertification of the working ability of the team and the dog's health is required by FSDI. Either the Roches visit the graduate's home or the team comes to them for an evaluation of the maintenance of the team's effectiveness.

Mike and P.J. describe themselves as dog advocates. Although their mission is to provide trained dogs to assist disabled people, they maintain a primary interest in the well-being of their dogs. Some disabled people, like some pet owners, see only the glamour of living with a well-trained dog and fail to reckon with the mundane aspects of dog ownership. Even though graduates have been counseled about the pros and cons of living with dogs, some people cannot cope with shedding, cleaning up feces, feeding schedules, grooming, play times, veterinary care and all the other aspects of routine management dogs require.

Dogs for the Deaf

As Toni was growing up in New York City, she fantasized about a life in which she would have lions, tigers and elephants as pets and playmates. For Toni, wild animals were part of her imaginary family. For Robin Dickson, Executive Director of Dogs for the Deaf (DFD), an extended wild animal family was a reality. Robin's dad, Roy Kabat, owned and operated Jungle Land near Hollywood, California, where animal actors resided when they weren't at the studios working in television or movies. From the time she was able to walk, Robin learned to work with and train many different animals. After her parents' divorce, Robin moved to the Midwest with her mother, who managed a boarding kennel and grooming service.

Roy, after his retirement from Jungle Land, became a consultant for the American Humane Association (AHA) in Denver, Colorado, when they began investigating the possibility of training dogs for the deaf and hard of hearing. One of his major recommendations, now common practice, was the training of dogs in a simulated apartment setting to approximate real life conditions. Dogs, who would be living and working in homes with their deaf partners, needed to be exposed to common household noises such as running water, dishwashers, garbage disposals, flushing toilets and slamming doors. Working with the AHA gave Roy the impetus to establish DFD in 1977, the oldest continuous training program for hearing dogs in the United States.

After completing her college education and teaching for twelve years, Robin moved to Oregon to assist her dad with DFD. For the next two years, she worked as an apprentice trainer and was then qualified as a certified audio canine trainer. In 1989, several years

Hearing dog trainee Austin, a Spaniel cross, learns to respond to a ringing telephone at Dogs for the Deaf.   Courtesy of DFD

after the death of her father, Robin and DFD moved to Central Point, Oregon, ten miles from the nearby town of Medford.

Since its inception, the program has graduated approximately 450 dogs. Suitable hearing dog candidates are obtained from animal shelters within a five to six hour driving distance from headquarters.

One of the most distressing aspects of the job for Robin and her staff is rejecting so many healthy, appealing dogs who do not have the desired qualities to become hearing dogs.

Since hearing dogs must alert their human partners by making physical contact, suitable candidates must weigh under thirty pounds. In addition, they should be younger than fourteen months, energetic, playful, friendly and self-confident. If dogs under eight months old are recruited, they are placed in puppy-raising homes. DFD recruits both males and females and all are neutered.

In the past, fifty percent of recruited dogs did not graduate as hearing dogs. Presently, very few dogs fail to be placed by DFD. Initially, all dogs are trained to alert to a ringing telephone, a knock at the door, a screeching smoke alarm, a buzzing alarm clock, a beeping oven timer or microwave and a whistling tea kettle. Dogs who master this training and demonstrate the ability to remain calm in public places are placed as certified hearing dogs with deaf partners. These hearing dogs have the same legal rights of access as guide dogs.

Dogs who respond well to their sound alert training but do not respond well in public settings are placed as working companion dogs. As such, they alert their deaf partners to sounds within the home but do not have the right of public access. Mellow and low-energy dogs, who do not respond well to the sound alert work, are placed as social dogs. Deaf children, too young to be partnered with a hearing dog, can have the companionship of a social dog while learning pet care and responsibility. Other social dogs go to homes of elderly or lonely people in need of a well-trained pet. Regardless of the category, all dogs trained by DFD go through an intensive obedience course. Because of this variety of placements, very few recruits are rejected by the program.

Robin's training staff consists of three certified audio canine trainers and two apprentices. Trainers are remarkably dedicated to their work since the financial rewards are marginal—the average salary is under $18,000 a year. On an annual operating budget of

$450,000, DFD graduates fifty dogs a year. An expansion program is underway and the goal is to double the graduation rate in the near future.

After four to six months of training, dogs are ready to be placed with their deaf or hard of hearing partners. An applicant desiring to be teamed with a hearing dog must be over eighteen and must submit an audiogram with a completed application. A volunteer committee of physicians and other professionals knowledgeable about deafness meets on a monthly basis to review applications. If accepted by this committee, the applicant receives a home visit from a staff member, a former graduate or a volunteer associated with the program. After a final evaluation, those who are accepted may have to wait as long as a year before meeting their special canine partner. Those applying for a successor dog are placed at the top of the waiting list.

When making the match, trainers try to respect the applicant's preference for the dog's size and gender. If an applicant expresses a special need, such as being alerted to a baby crying, the dog selected for that person will be trained to respond to that sound during the final weeks of training.

DFD trainers travel throughout the United States to place certified hearing dogs and working companion dogs in their new homes at no expense to the deaf partner. For a certified hearing dog, the training time is five days with the team; for a working companion, the training time is three days. With both placements, the deaf partner is taught to understand how the dog alerts to sounds in the home and how to maintain obedience training and care for the dog's grooming and health-related needs. As part of this training process, the working partners are introduced to their new veterinarian. Since certified hearing dogs have public access rights, extra time is allocated to work with the team in shopping centers, restaurants and on public transportation.

During the in-home training period, a bond begins to grow between the human and canine partners. Everything is done to encourage this process. After an intensive and emotional day of training, the team is left to relax and play at home while the trainer spends the night at a nearby hotel. To facilitate communication with trainees who use sign language, all trainers have taken courses in American Sign Language.

In the course of our interview with Robin, she told us about Hellen Sneddon, a woman from our hometown of Fresno, California, who received a DFD hearing dog in September, 1990. We phoned Hellen and, with the assistance of the California Relay service, spoke with her about Myra.

Hellen and her hearing husband did a great deal of traveling by motor home and belonged to the Good Sam Club, a major fund-raising group for DFD. It was not until Hellen's husband died that she began thinking about getting a hearing dog. She describes Myra as a bundle of energy who keeps her busy. Hellen lovingly boasts that Myra is a hard little worker, a great companion and a real sweet-heart. It was a love affair at first sight that grows deeper with each day. Hellen says she is very proud of this little dog who has brought her peace of mind and a feeling of security. She no longer worries about missing telephone calls, the doorbell or someone calling her from another part of the house. She can now sleep well at night knowing Myra would awaken her if the smoke alarm went off or some other emergency materialized.

Myra has two cats as playmates. DFD, like most programs training hearing dogs, will not place a trainee in a home with pet dogs. The rationale for this position is that hearing dogs primarily work in the home and could be distracted by the presence of pet dogs.

San Francisco SPCA Hearing Dog Program

In 1978, the San Francisco Society for Prevention of Cruelty to Animals (SFSPCA) was one of the pioneers in establishing a hearing dog program. Staff members travel throughout northern and central California searching for suitable shelter recruits to do this important work. Like DFD, trainers look for young, outgoing, trainable dogs.

Dogs who pass these initial tests are brought back to the SFSPCA for further testing and training. Their new home for the next four months will be kennels built on the roof of this renowned San Francisco institution. Through an initial veterinary check-up, dogs with medical problems are eliminated from the training pool. Dogs eliminated at this stage or any succeeding stage of training are placed at the SFSPCA shelter for adoption.

On the day we observed the program, Molly, a recent recruit, was being trained to respond to a knock on the door and the ring of

Mark Barnes and Laney, his hearing dog partner, relax in a park near the Golden Gate bridge. Laney was rescued and trained by the San Francisco SPCA Hearing Dog Program.
Courtesy of SFSPCA

a telephone. Martha Hoffman and Kathy O'Brien, two of the three trainers, worked together in trying to get this Terrier mix to respond properly. Martha held Molly on leash while Kathy stood several feet away. Kathy placed a ringing telephone on the floor, squatted down and called Molly to her. A piece of food was placed on the ringing telephone to reward Molly for responding to this sound. Martha then recalled Molly, guiding her in with the lead. A hearing dog alerts his/her deaf or hard of hearing partner by making physical contact, then running to the source of the sound. Barking is ineffective and, therefore, discouraged as a means of signaling. Molly had obviously been trained not to jump on people by her former owner because she was reluctant to make body contact with Martha, who was trying to entice her to do so. After several trials, Molly gave in to the temptation of food rewards, verbal encouragement and praise. Ralph Dennard, CEO, explained that extinguishing this early training in good manners is a common problem faced by his training staff.

Deaf people use telephones by employing a device called Text Telephone (TT). This device permits deaf people to communicate using the written word rather than the voice. Two deaf people with this equipment converse by dialing the phone number in the usual manner, typing the message on a standard keyboard that is transmitted via telephone and printed out on paper or a screen. The receiver of the call then types her/his message and the conversation continues. Hearing persons contact deaf people or vice versa by dialing a specially designated number and communicating through a third party. These relay operators convert the spoken message of the hearing person into writing on their Text Telephones for the deaf person and vice versa. Because this process takes longer than verbal communication, reduced telephone rates are available to those who use this equipment.

Although vibrating alarm clocks are available for those who cannot hear a ringing or buzzing alarm, a hearing dog is a much more effective waker-upper! At the sound of the alarm, the dog jumps on the bed to awaken his/her deaf partner with licks and nuzzles. Another very important unheard sound is the smoke alarm. Whether the partner is awake or asleep, the hearing dog gets attention through physical contact, then maintains a Sit Stay. By gaining the deaf partner's attention and not running toward the source of the sound, the dog cues his/her partner to the fact the smoke alarm has gone off.

A San Francisco SPCA Hearing Dog program trainer observes class obedience exercise.
Courtesy of SFSPCA

Deaf applicants for the SFSPCA Hearing Dog Program are interviewed in their homes. Staff members have a working knowledge of American Sign Language, but for the interview and at the time of training, professional interpreters are employed. An application fee of $20 is required, as well as a training fee of $100. This minimal payment demonstrates the personal investment of the applicant to the program as well as contributing toward the estimated $10,000 it costs to train a team. Preference is given to those who live alone or with other deaf people, are over sixteen and do not have pet dogs in the home. If a deaf person lives with a hearing person, the probability is the hearing person will take away the function of the dog by answering the door or telephone or by indicating an alarm has gone off.

Successful applicants travel to San Francisco at their own expense and stay at a nearby motel at the expense of the Hearing Dog Program. Local residents commute from their homes. During the week-long training period, trainees are matched with their new canine partners and learn how to handle obedience and sound-response training. They attend lectures on dog behavior and learn about the medical, grooming and social needs of their dogs.

Each trainee is provided with a crate to ensure the dog's good behavior at the motel and later at home. No time is spent on housebreaking these rescued dogs and therefore the crates help the deaf partners deal with this chore. Like guide and service dogs, hearing dogs must be continuously reinforced in their training in order to maintain a high degree of effectiveness.

In the twelve years of its existence, this program has trained 350 teams. Part of the estimated $10,000 cost of training a team is reflected in the commitment to provide free veterinary care for graduates who can be brought to the SFSPCA veterinary hospital for care. This figure also reflects the commitment to visit the partners after they return home. Early intervention by the training staff when problems of adjustment are reported can prevent these problems from becoming major and disrupting the working relationship.

Southeastern Guide Dogs

Southeastern has its origins in the early 1980s. Robert Miller, an active member of the Lions Club, wanted to establish a guide dog school in Florida. Before the establishment of Southeastern, blind Southerners had to train at guide dog schools in the North. Bob realized several problems could be solved by having a guide dog school located in the South. Northern-bred and reared dogs often had difficulty adjusting to climatic and environmental conditions with skin problems and flea allergies abounding. Northern dogs received training primarily in urban areas; blind Southerners wanted more training in suburban and rural conditions. In addition, a school located in the South could provide more immediate aftercare services. Based on these considerations, he raised funds from friends and Lions Club members, incorporated Southeastern as a nonprofit organization in November 1982 and hired Mike Sergeant, then working for Pilot Dogs to join the program as Director of Training and CEO.

Mike grew up on a farm in upstate New York, where farm and pet animals were part of everyday life. Given this background, it was only natural for him to become a dog handler while serving in the military during the Vietnam War. He worked with attack, search and rescue and sniffer dogs. Wanting to continue a career in dogs after his discharge in 1972, he successfully applied for a job as an apprentice trainer at Guiding Eyes for the Blind. Eight years later he went to work for Pilot Dogs until he assumed leadership of Southeastern in 1983.

For the first few years, Mike and his family lived in rented quarters and Southeastern existed on a shoestring budget. As time went by and Bob became less and less involved in the program, other members of the Lions Club assumed more active roles. Of these, Harris Silverman, a Bradenton ophthalmologist, has had the greatest influence.

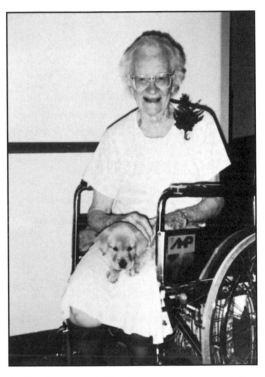

At Southeastern Guide Dogs, puppy hugging brings joy to both humans and canines.
Courtesy of Southeastern Guide Dogs

Harris, currently serving as president of Southeastern's board, was the driving force behind the purchase of property and construction of a modern guide dog school facility in Palmetto. Realizing surgery and medication could not save everyone's vision, Harris devoted himself to raising funds for a program offering independent mobility to patients going blind. His wife Micheline, who shares his love of dogs and commitment to blind people, serves as secretary of the board.

According to Harris, Southeastern is run like a lean machine. With a 1991 budget of $713,000, South-eastern graduated ninety-five teams. At an average team cost of $8,000, this program has one of the lowest costs per guide dog team of any school in the United States.

From the start, Southeastern has relied heavily on an extended network of volunteers. Florida, with its large population of retirees, provides an ideal environment for the utilization of the skills and services of a diverse group of people. When the school was housed in a three-bedroom home, volunteers provided all of the meals and invited students to their homes. Despite the construction of a dormitory and an increase in class size to twelve students, community participation has been maintained and encouraged.

Mike, conscious of cost containment, is proud that Southeastern can feed a class in residence for twenty-six days at an average cost of $550. Food is donated by food-processing companies, local supermarkets, fast food franchises and local farmers also donate to the cause. Volunteers continue to provide lunches. Service clubs sponsor outings and invite students for meals.

Construction costs have also been kept down due to the generosity of local builders who have completed the $335,000 dormitory/administration complex and the $285,000 Bradenton training lounge at cost. These buildings are now owned outright by Southeastern Guide Dogs. Puppy raisers are invited to observe their formerly silly, playful, awkward, adolescent puppies now working as serious, mature guides partnered with blind people. During the second weekend of class, Southeastern hosts a get-together where puppy raisers and blind students have the opportunity to meet, socialize and exchange dog stories.

Volunteers who cannot foster puppies for a year can still reap the benefits of puppy love. Puppy "huggers" visit the kennel to play with puppies before they leave for their new homes. Dog walkers provide extra love and attention to the sixty kenneled dogs during their four- to six-month training period.

Volunteers even play a role in the application process. Ideally, a trainer is sent to each applicant's home for a personal interview and evaluation lasting two to three hours. However, where this is not possible, a volunteer, usually someone involved in the puppy raising program and familiar with Southeastern's policies, will conduct the interview. Recognizing that a contributing factor to the success of the working team is the attitude of family members and employers, the interviewer makes every attempt to involve them in the application process. Applicants are informed of their responsibilities as guide dog partners. They are told it will cost them between $600 to $800 a year to provide food, semi-annual veterinary visits, heartworm medication and flea and tick control for their new partners.

As a regional program, Southeastern only accepts applications from southern residents. Within the southern population, Floridians are given preference in the application process. Floridians, constituting seventy-five percent of the graduate body, have an average eight-month wait before beginning training compared with a one-year wait for other Southerners. Applicants must be seventeen or older, but Mike will consider younger applicants on a case-by-case basis. A fifteen-year-old youngster from Texas has been accepted for training with the provision that his father spends the one month training period with him. At the other end of the age spectrum, ten percent of applicants accepted for training are over age seventy-five, and Southeastern takes pride in having a graduate in his late eighties.

Remaining committed to the goal of training dogs to work in a southern environment, Southeastern emphasizes suburban and rural travel techniques. Most students will be matched with Labrador Retrievers, while others will be matched with Australian Shepherds, Smooth Collies, German Shepherd Dogs or Labrador/Golden Retriever crosses. When designing the student dining room, Mike set up a clever configuration simulating a restaurant. Students and their dogs experience dining at round tables, square tables, booths and a counter with stools. Whatever the configuration, dogs must lie quietly under the table, under the chair or alongside the partner's seat.

A close relationship has been developed with eight local veterinarians who donate their services and act as specialist-consultants. Southeastern also has a working relationship with the veterinary schools located in Florida, Alabama and Georgia. These institutions charge Southeastern only for their out-of-pocket cost.

More than 300 teams have been graduated in less than a decade and 171 are still working. The graduation goal of 120 teams a year is close to being realized.

Leaving Florida, we were feeling the effects of being on eight planes in eleven days. After dozing for most of the trip, we got up to stretch our legs and use the facilities. Ivy and Kirby were asleep under the seats in front of us, a place generally used for carry-on luggage. Apparently, during the few minutes we were away, an unexpected adventure took place. The passenger seated in front of Toni placed an open box of expensive cookies under her seat, not realizing an insatiable Golden Retriever was already there. Imagine Ivy's delight when, without having to move a muscle, she was offered this delectable treat! Imagine the passenger's consternation when, reaching under her seat for a cookie, she found an empty box! Fortunately, Ivy showed no ill effects from her gluttony.

Guide Dog Foundation

As part of the American Airlines-sponsored tour of guide dog schools, we visited the Guide Dog Foundation for the Blind in Smithtown, New York. You may have seen or heard their marvelous radio and television public service announcements featuring guide dogs in a variety of situations. William Shatner, Ed Asner and Betty White are among the celebrities who have contributed their time and talent to these educational spots. These announcements have not only helped educate the public about the role of guide dogs in society, but have also had an unanticipated dividend for the Foundation. Two of the students in the class we visited chose to apply to this school after hearing these announcements.

The Foundation, founded more than forty years ago, graduated fifty-nine teams in 1991. Labrador and Golden Retrievers are bred by

Puppy raisers return their canine charges to Guide Dog Foundation. After a year of tender loving care and socialization, young dogs will be evaluated and begin their formal guide dog training.   Courtesy of Guide Dog Foundation

the Foundation and are trained for from three to six months before meeting their new partners. Typical class size is twelve students working with two instructors and an apprentice.

When Toni worked at KPPC, she frequently visited friends getting guide dogs at the nearby Smithtown-based Foundation. However, Ed had never toured the facility. CEO Wells Jones spent several hours with us and showed us around the newly-renovated student residence. Wells had previously been a senior staff member at United Cerebral Palsy of New York City. Although he has spent most of his working career in the rehabilitation field, he especially enjoys observing the rapid transformation in the lives of blind people resulting from the month long stay at the Foundation. In his opinion, "Trading the cane for a guide dog makes a big difference in the student's sense of independence and mobility."

Guide Dog Foundation Board President Heidi Vandewinckel takes a moment out of her busy work day to show appreciation for her guide dog, Murphy.
Courtesy of Guide Dog Foundation

Wells is making every attempt to be responsive to the needs of students and graduates. Two guide dog partners sit on the Board of Directors. In response to graduate input, many new policies have been instituted and many other changes are under consideration. A new computer system has been installed permitting the staff to correspond with applicants and graduates in braille or large print formats. To further facilitate communication, an 800 telephone line has been installed.

We were impressed with the innovative idea of having credit card telephones in each student's room, in addition to a pay-phone for general use in the library. Living away from home for the month of training is emotionally draining for many people. Privacy is limited and phone calls from the public booth must be kept short to accommodate others.

Although many schools are trying to recruit older students, few are focused on the needs of mothers with young children. We were told about a nursing mother whose request for a guide dog had been rejected by many other programs. Recognizing her special circumstances, the Foundation was willing to accommodate her needs. Her husband and children stayed in a nearby hotel and, working around the training and lecture schedule, she was able to continue nursing her infant. Citing this example and the phone system allowing students to remain close to the folks back home, Wells emphasized the Foundation's commitment to personalized service and flexibility.

Another innovative program designed for puppy raisers is Camp Guide Dog, which meets one Saturday a month on the school grounds. Participants can work with the training staff and get the benefit of collective expertise on any problems they may be facing with their puppies. These gatherings generate a sense of camaraderie among puppy raisers. Pleased with this development, the Foundation is placing puppies from the same litter in the same geographic area to foster group interaction. At the suggestion of graduates, the Foundation has re-instituted a puppy raiser reception. On the third Sunday of class, raisers, financial sponsors and members of the students' families are invited to meet one another and mingle with the students.

Innovations at the Foundation also extend to the training staff. This is the only school whose instructors and apprentices are unionized. As members of the United Auto Workers Union, they work under a collectively bargained contract. An apprentice starts at $18,000; instructors receive $24,000 and, after eight years' experience, earn $33,000. Fringe benefits are part of the contract package. The salaries quoted above are based on a forty-hour work week at the time this book was written. When classes are in session, instructors put in a great deal of overtime and can earn $40,000 a year or more.

Leader Dogs

If we told you we flew to Michigan to meet some lions would you think we were traveling to the Detroit Zoo? We weren't. The lions we visited were not ferocious and, in fact, were charming. These lions had gone to the dogs! They were members of the staff of the Leader Dogs for the Blind school in Rochester, Michigan. This school, founded in 1938, was established by members of the Lions clubs of America. A close relationship between Leader and the Lions has persisted for the last fifty years.

Art Fleming, an instructor and team leader, met us at the Detroit airport to escort us to the school. Ivy and Kirby have experienced all sorts of working conditions: construction, elevators, escalators, subways, ferry boats and busy street crossings. However, we had never encountered an automatic revolving door. The revolving doors familiar to us were manually controlled. At the Detroit airport, the revolving door is electronically operated with two speeds, fast and faster. When we approached this potentially lethal device, we halted and waited for Art to give us the signal to proceed. With thoughts of crushed fingers and mangled paws, we entered this madly spinning apparatus and magically came out unharmed at the other end! Despite our apprehension, the dogs handled this encounter as they do most new experiences in our partnership, with aplomb.

When we made arrangements to visit Leader, the largest guide dog school, we were invited to live in the student dormitory. We stayed in a comfortable room furnished with twin beds, two desks, a double closet and a private bathroom. Meals were served in the student and staff dining room.

The morning after our arrival, we met with CEO Bill Hansen. Bill, a gregarious, retired Air Force colonel, assumed the presidency of Leader in 1988. His varied background in public relations, management and education led to his selection as CEO. Getting this job was the closest thing to fulfilling his childhood fantasy of becoming a country doctor.

Observing Bill at his desk handling problems from the front office, fielding questions from us and interacting with members of his staff, it is difficult to imagine that he was a novice at this dog business just four years ago. He was not a Lion, his only dog experience was with his fifteen-year-old Poodle and he was not familiar with the problems of blindness. He is now an active member of the Lions Club, has added two Golden Retrievers to his household and has familiarized himself with the problems faced by blind people.

Leader Dog team in training boards a bus. Because guide dogs are permitted on public transportation, learning good bus riding manners is an important part of training.
Courtesy of Leader Dogs for the Blind

After our morning session with Bill, we had lunch with the training staff and spent the afternoon at the school's lounge in downtown Rochester. This facility is used by students and instructors when they are not actually on the streets training.

These dedicated instructors will let almost nothing interfere with the training process. Neither wind, nor rain, nor snow keeps these Leader trainers from their appointed rounds. When it snows in Rochester, a common occurrence during the winter, trainers take on the responsibility of snow removal from routes traveled by teams in the early stages of training. During the winter the Leader switchboard is deluged by calls from local residents requesting clearance of their sidewalks!

Leader not only has graduated teams working in almost every state, it also has an international presence. Of the 2,077 teams currently working, 471 are outside the United States. Spain and Canada account for almost 400 of them, but they are found in Denmark, Israel, Turkey and Morocco among other countries.

To facilitate their growing emphasis on quality, Leader is in the process of building a new complex. There will be a new kennel to house its 250 dogs in a better living environment, provision for the storage of maintenance equipment and dog food (Leader uses a staggering 140,000 pounds of dog food a year) and the basement will contain a conference room and a model apartment.

Dr. David Smith, staff veterinarian, and Dr. Gussie Eastman, Leader's semi-retired veterinarian who lives on the campus, are looking forward to an expanded and modern veterinary clinic in the new facility. These veterinarians routinely examine every dog once a month and are on call for emergency care around the clock. As part of team training, students and their canine partners experience visiting the on-campus veterinary clinic.

We were impressed with the friendliness, informality and dedication of those working for Leader and very appreciative of the many kindnesses and attention shown to us during our short visit. Many members of the training staff have been working for the school for more than fifteen years. Training activities take place throughout the year by five four-person training teams who train the dogs for four months and then foster the partnership between blind person and guide dog during the fifth month. Under Bill's direction, class size has been cut from thirty to twenty-four. In 1990, 303 teams

As part of Leader Dogs international outreach, trainees from Spain, accompanied by an interpreter, learn proper foot work in approaching a street crossing.

Courtesy of Leader Dogs for the Blind

were graduated and the projected figure for 1991 is even lower. The instructional staff's devotion to quality guide dog training is not based on lucrative salaries; an instructor with ten years of experience earns less than $30,000 annually.

One of Leader's four field representatives is blind. These reps travel around the country giving demonstrations, raising funds and interviewing potential applicants. Several other blind people work on a per diem basis representing Leader at conferences, giving talks and acting as liaison to other Leader graduates. One blind person is on the governing board. As consumer advocates, we would like to see more blind people employed by guide dog schools and serving on their boards of directors.

Paws With a Cause

Another Michigan-based program is Paws With a Cause. Founded in 1979 by Michael Sapp, it is headquartered in the little town of Byron Center, in the western part of the state. Initially, Mike trained

A young student trains his Paws With a Cause service dog to flip the light switch. Courtesy of Paws With a Cause

hearing dogs in his basement for local deaf residents. Like some other hearing dog programs, dogs were brought to their deaf partners' homes for final team training. As the physically disabled community became aware of the benefits of service dogs, Mike was asked to include them in his training program. As the need for service and hearing dogs expanded, Mike did not have the financial resources or staff to meet the demand. Therefore, he developed an innovative model permitting Paws to expand its services into other states without straining its financial resources.

Paws' approach is to educate dogs at the training center and then send the educated dogs home with their disabled partners to complete the training process. Dogs come from a variety of sources. The vast majority are shelter rescues, some are donated and a small percentage are bred by Paws and placed in puppy-raising homes. Golden and Labrador Retrievers are usually the breeds selected for the five- to seven-month service dog training program, while a variety of breeds and crosses are selected for the two- to four-month hearing dog program.

Disabled applicants are carefully screened, assessing their need for an assistance dog, emotional maturity and level of responsibility. This interviewing process is even more rigorous for children. Before applicants are interviewed in their homes, they must complete an extensive questionnaire. A major function of this questionnaire is to assess the applicant's knowledge about the costs and benefits of living with a dog. Does the applicant have a realistic idea of food and veterinary costs, the time and energy involved in grooming, flea control, taking the dog out for relief on a regular schedule in all kinds of weather and picking up feces? Armed with information from the questionnaire, the interviewer can discuss areas in which unrealistic expectations are expressed.

If at all possible, the successful applicant is expected to visit the training center to meet his/her prospective canine partner. If it turns out to be a case of love at first sight, the dog, who has already learned basic hearing or service dog commands, can now be trained to meet the applicant's individual needs. If the initial match does not seem to be working, other dogs in the kennel can be brought in until a good match is achieved.

All dogs are exposed to a variety of common assistance dog experiences. Cats are present at the training facility and are brought into the model apartment to accustom the dogs to them. The model apartment is used as a simulated home setting. This exposure is especially important for hearing dogs who will learn to alert their deaf partners to many common household sounds.

Mike believes the success of a working team depends on support for the disabled person and dog once they return home from the training facility. Concentrating on the transfer process, Mike employs fifty-five part-time field trainers to work with disabled partners and trained dogs in their home communities. As the team begins to bond and work together, the field trainer visits in the team's home once or twice a week. The disabled partner is coached on dog behavior, voice control, praise and correction, grooming and veterinary care. Crate use is encouraged to maintain housetraining and to avoid problems such as chewing.

As the team meets with success in the home, the field trainer accompanies them in the community to shops, malls, restaurants, theaters, schools, medical facilities or wherever the team wants to go. The field trainer also works with the team on public transportation if desired.

When the field trainer and disabled person think the team is a safe and reliable functioning unit, the disabled person applies for certification. Usually, this process takes six months to a year. Certification is either done by the field trainer or by one of the fifteen regional training directors employed by Paws. Both hearing and service dogs must demonstrate exemplary behavior in public places. In addition, both must alert to the smoke alarm. Hearing dogs must alert to the sound of an intruder and service dogs must demonstrate the ability to retrieve a portable telephone. Beyond these basics, dogs must demonstrate mastery of tasks unique to their disabled partners' needs. If the team fails the certification test, the disabled person is given additional time to work on those areas needing improvement. In some cases, teams never reach the level of proficiency considered necessary for certification. If the team does not qualify, the dog returns to Paws with a Cause.

Once a team is certified, Paws gives the disabled person ownership of the dog. Help and support are always available. This policy is based on the belief that if a good relationship exists between Paws and its graduates, there is no reason to maintain the power to reclaim a certified dog. When a problem cannot be solved, such as aggression, certification, not the dog, is withdrawn.

Paws With a Cause service dog Nikki helps his partner Joan Froling with the groceries.
Courtesy of Joan Froling

Graduate Joan Froling, partnered with Samoyed service dog Nikki, is enthusiastic about the Paws program. Nikki not only represents an unusual assistance dog breed, but also an unusual Paws graduate. Nikki was Joan's pet dog and continues to be shown in AKC conformation competition.

Nikki has mastered more than fifty task-oriented commands. Most of the specialized tasks he performs for Joan are based on his ability to retrieve and carry. One of these is helping with the groceries, which are packed in canvas bags with Velcro fasteners. When Joan arrives home from the store, she places the bags on the ground. After he helps Joan get into the house, Nikki carries in the bags one at a time. He unloads the bags and places the items one at a time on Joan's lap for her to put in the refrigerator or cupboards. On pickup days Nikki carries bags of garbage to the curb. When the doorbell rings, Nikki acts as Joan's butler. He opens the door and escorts the guest to Joan.

All Paws dogs are trained to alert to the sound of the smoke alarm. If Joan is in bed when the smoke alarm goes off, Nikki will bring Joan her walker so she can get up. He will then retrieve her cane so she can get to her electric cart. His next task is opening the door so she can safely exit the house.

For Joan, one of the incredible things about having a service dog is traveling alone without the necessity of being accompanied by a family member. Prior to her first trip accompanied only by Nikki, Joan made arrangements with Northwest Airlines for permission to board an airplane not in use to familiarize Nikki with boarding procedures. Under the supervision of her field trainer, Nikki demonstrated his confidence and competence with his role as flight escort. Northwest also benefitted from the experience and subsequently provided Paws foster puppies and dogs in training with a similar experience at the Detroit Metropolitan Airport.

The Paws model of having field trainers working with trained dogs and disabled partners in their homes over several months intrigues us. As guide dog partners, we know most problems arise shortly after the blind person and canine partner return home following a month of training at a residential facility. If the guide dog schools incorporated some features of this model by cutting down on the time spent at the school and worked with competent dog trainers in the blind person's community, we believe the transition from school to home would be easier and the number of guide dogs returned within one year of graduation would greatly decrease.

Chapter Four

The People Behind the Scenes: Puppy Raisers

Up to this point, we have focused on training programs and the activities of trainers. All of their activities, however, depend upon the uncompensated service provided by dedicated volunteers. Within this class of people who support the assistance dog movement through the sweat of their brows and a commitment to helping others, puppy raisers are an indispensable element. All programs breeding their own candidates for work, as well as those recruiting young dogs from shelters, depend upon the loving homes provided by these dedicated volunteers.

In 1989 and 1990 we traveled to the United Kingdom to study the guide dog movement in that country. Guide Dogs for the Blind Association (GDBA) in the United Kingdom is the largest guide dog program in the

There's nothing more delightful than a lap full of puppies. Courtesy of GDBA

world. Although GDBA and American schools both utilize puppy raisers, many differences exist.

This British puppy raiser shares a magic moment with her young charge. Courtesy of GDBA

A Comparison of Methods

Ed had always regretted not meeting Perrier's puppy raisers. At some guide dog schools, including The Seeing Eye™ where Ed trained with Perrier, puppy raisers and blind students never meet. The only information given to the puppy raiser is the occupation and home state of the blind partner while the graduate receives no information about his or her dog's puppy raiser. At Guide Dogs of the Desert, where Ed trained with Kirby, puppy raisers and blind students meet at a graduation ceremony. Several American guide dog schools follow the GDD model. In the United Kingdom, students are given the names and addresses of their puppy raisers and encouraged to contact them. Many long-term friendships in both countries have begun this way.

Kirby's puppy raisers, Barbara and Roger Melanson, like thousands of other devoted puppy raisers, are a crucial element in the success of the guide dog movement. Kirby was twelve weeks old when he went to live with the Melansons. This bundle of Golden Retriever joy had to be housetrained and taught house manners. Chewing shoes and other household items, tearing up garbage and chasing the family cat were forbidden activities. Kirby was taught to ride quietly in the family car and, of course, like any well-trained dog, was taught basic obedience. He was taken on country walks as well as exposed to typical city noises, traffic and crowds. Through frequent contact with Barbara and Roger's grandchildren, Kirby learned gentleness and the joy of joining in children's games.

Historically in the United States, guide dog puppy raising has been a major project of 4-H Clubs where children, supervised by adult volunteer leaders, take on this activity as a club project. In the United Kingdom, only adults are recruited as puppy raisers and they are supervised by paid staff members.

GDBA is a nationwide organization with seven large regional training centers and a number of smaller satellites. The British have one program, in contrast to the fourteen U.S. programs, and since the U.K. is much smaller, the GDBA is able to establish certain policies which would not be possible in America. Puppy raisers volunteer their services directly to a GDBA regional center and must live within a radius of fifty miles. Organized group activities are not an essential part of the program. Each raiser is visited once a month by the supervisor, and together they take the puppy into a nearby town to evaluate his or her reactions to an urban environment. In this fashion, problems can be discovered early and steps can be taken to remedy them.

In the U.S., puppies are approximately ten weeks old when sent to live with their raisers. In the U.K., every attempt is made to place puppies in new homes at the age of six weeks. British puppies are taken from their dams, brought to the center for a physical examination and placed in foster homes the next day. The British believe early and continuous interaction with people in a home setting instills people-oriented behavioral patterns. They believe a puppy left with its littermates and dam longer than six weeks learns dog-oriented behavior patterns which they feel are less important for future guide dogs. Thinking in the U.S. is somewhat different. A dam and her litter usually stay together for more than six weeks and puppies are evaluated for a week or two while being kenneled at the schools before being placed in a home setting.

Good puppy raising is the foundation of a well-mannered working guide dog, but in our experience, many American puppy raisers are not familiar with the training and duties of a working guide. The raiser may live a considerable distance from the school providing the puppy and may never have contact with a blind person/guide dog team. Because British puppy raisers live no more than an hour's drive from a training center, they are in close contact with the center and its training program. In addition, British puppy raisers are encouraged to join their local GDBA fund-raising branch, which usually includes several guide dog partners.

Success rate is measured by the proportion of dogs bred by the school and puppies raised who graduate as working guides or are selected as breeding stock. This rate varies significantly between the two countries. GDBA's rate is eighty percent compared with fifty percent for most American schools. How much of this greater success is due to the differences in breeding practices we are not qualified to judge. However, we firmly believe much of the greater success can be attributed to the differences in the puppy raising programs.

People frequently ask how puppy raisers can give up dogs they have loved and cherished for more than a year. Even though they know it is going to happen, the break is truly traumatic for most people. Our cat sitter, Candie Wasson, began raising guide dog puppies at the age of eleven. When we went to England in August, 1989, Candie was returning her eleventh puppy to Guide Dogs for the Blind. Like many raisers, Candie was ambivalent. She wanted Heron to succeed as a guide, but loved her and hoped she would fail. When puppies do not qualify as guides, they are usually offered to their raisers as pets. If the raisers cannot keep them, they are offered as pets to people who have placed their names on waiting lists at the schools. Usually a donation is expected in exchange for receiving a well-behaved and well-trained dog. Other dogs, called career change dogs, may go into police work, search and rescue work or therapy work at a nursing home or similar facility. In rare cases they may be retrained as service dogs.

Now that she was in her mid-twenties, Candie told us Heron was the last puppy she would raise. However, when we returned from the U.K., Candie introduced us to Manda, her new Golden Retriever puppy. She sighed with resignation, explaining that raising guide dog puppies was addictive. Guide dog schools effectively foster this addiction by giving a young puppy to the raiser to replace a dog who is being returned to begin training.

We witnessed a wonderful transformation at the last 4-H Club field day we attended. A teen-aged girl was sobbing as she handed over the leash of the dog she had raised for the past year. Her tears turned to laughter as the puppy placed in her arms began licking away her tears.

Another view of this addictive process was obtained in the U.K., where a puppy raiser shared her experience. She and her husband had several pet dogs. As these dogs aged and subsequently died, her family went through the grief of pet loss. Now, raising her eighteenth puppy for GDBA, she enjoyed the opportunity of working and living with young dogs and avoiding the trauma of pet aging and loss. She took great pride in informing us that fifteen of her puppies had made it as guides or breeding stock. In her case, and that of many other British puppy raisers, direct knowledge of the function of a guide dog engenders a sense of pride and accomplishment we feel is absent for many American puppy raisers. For instance, when Barbara and Roger were leaving after their visit, they said they had never seen a working team and had no idea what Kirby's life was like at home when he was not working.

Joanna Walker

Joanna Walker is a remarkable woman with a mission. This sixty-nine-year-old North Carolina resident has committed considerable funds and a great deal of time in promoting the image of the Doberman Pinscher as guide dog.

While growing up in England, Joanna had a variety of pets. One condition of pet ownership insisted upon by her parents was full responsibility for the animals. Litter boxes were to be kept clean, horses were to be groomed, rabbits were to be fed, dogs were to be walked—in short, all the care for Joanna's pets had to come from her. Her parents insisted upon well-mannered pets and, although obedience classes were not common in those days, her mother tutored her on dog training techniques. As a result, Joanna's family's dogs traveled everywhere with the family.

From earliest childhood, Joanna had a burning desire to train guide dogs. This desire was fanned by a close family friend—a German Shepherd Dog breeder who donated several bitches from each litter to GDBA. As a young adult, Joanna wanted to translate this desire to be a guide dog trainer into a career. However, her World War II work assignment was in the secretarial field. Then, in 1947, she married an American and moved to the United States.

After months of socialization and training, Joanna Walker returns Star to begin her formal guide dog training at Pilot Dogs.
Courtesy of Joanna Walker

Although Joanna had no direct contact with Dobermans, she fell in love with the breed when she saw one in a film. Her most treasured wedding gift was a Dobe puppy. This initial pet partnership led to a lifelong love affair with the breed. Beginning in the early 1950s, the Walkers began breeding, showing, competing in Obedience Trials and doing their share in the rescue effort for Dobermans, making a permanent impact on the history of the breed.

Joanna's early interest in guide dogs was rekindled when a childhood friend, Nell, went blind in her thirtys. Initially, Nell would have nothing to do with guide dogs, but with Joanna's persistent encouragement, she trained with a dog at GDBA and has become a committed guide dog partner. On Joanna's visits back to England, she observed the almost magical performance of this human/dog partnership and learned some of the basics of training and performance.

Fantasizing about combining her love of Dobermans with her interest in guide dogs, she and Keith visited the Columbus, Ohio–based Pilot Dog training center. Pilot, the only guide dog school training Dobermans, recruited its future guides from donated stock. Pilot's executive director was impressed with the quality of the Walkers' show dogs, but regretted they were too big for his program.

In the early 1980s, Joanna Walker got involved with Doberman rescue. When a small, red puppy bitch was found, Joanna recognized her potential as a future Pilot dog. She placed Red in a foster home for six months, then embarked on a course of training, preparing her to work as a future guide.

The puppy had been well socialized in the foster home but Joanna continued to expose her to real life situations, such as noisy traffic, shopping malls, children at play and the presence of other animals. Joanna refutes the stereotype of the Doberman as an unfriendly, dangerous dog. She claims that given a proper upbringing, this breed can be curious, friendly and outgoing.

Putting Red on a Sit Stay and encouraging curious onlookers to pet this sweet canine was part of her training regimen. Her reasoning was simple. If a dog can be petted by strangers without becoming unruly, the acceptance of other people would be maintained while remaining under the handler's control. Subsequently, the blind partner might continue this petting-permissive behavior or discontinue it.

When Red was brought to Pilot, the staff was impressed with the extent of her early training and socialization. Requiring little in the way of additional formal training, Red was soon matched with her blind partner. Following the success of this initial venture, Joanna worked closely with Pilot on honing her skills.

Joanna is relentless in her testing of future guides. Shy, aggressive or otherwise unsuitable dogs are immediately rejected and good homes are found for them. With her extensive background with this breed, Joanna relies heavily on her powers of observation to select potential candidates for training. Of the more than thirty dogs Joanna has selected in the last twelve years, some come from her own breeding, some are donated by other reputable breeders and some are rescued.

She places young puppies in foster homes for approximately six months before honing their future skills. Usually, only one dog at a time is with her. She travels everywhere with her dog-in-training and has encountered an open door policy from local merchants, restaurant owners, theater managers and airport security. Joanna's dogs learn to work on escalators and through revolving doors, to handle crowds in malls and to lie quietly in restaurants and during theatrical performances. In addition, they are taught to lie on the floor of a car and to find the check-out counter in a market.

The young Dobermans are taken to obedience classes where they are able to socialize with dogs from a variety of other breeds. Since guide dogs must be aware of their total environment, Joanna does not teach them to focus on her face while participating in the training exercises, nor does she demand from her dogs the precision of trial competition.

The Dobes brought to Pilot by Joanna are in excellent health, neutered and up-to-date in their shots. Costs for these services are met by the Walkers. Joanna is proud that every one of the more than thirty dogs she has turned over to Pilot has graduated as a guide.

Admitting she occasionally has thoughts of going somewhere unencumbered by one of her youthful canine proteges, Joanna's sense of commitment and responsibility causes her to veto these natural inclinations. As a trainer, she knows every experience can be transformed into a learning opportunity. The pup learns to maintain a Down Stay while she tries on clothing during a shopping expedition. When grocery shopping, the trainee learns to walk quietly without sniffing. During meetings of Joanna's dog training club and local humane society, the future guide learns to lie quietly under the table. Nursing home patients benefit from visits with the young Dobes and the dogs become comfortable around wheelchairs, crutches and walkers.

Joanna proudly insists that once a blind person experiences partnership with a Doberman guide, an immediate and life-long commitment to the breed ensues.

Eve Hoopes

When Eve Hoopes rings the doorbell, our dogs go nuts. We tell them to Platform. At this command, our three Goldens do a Down Stay on the stair platform leading to the second floor of our town house. Observing the level of excitement when released, you might think Eve had a case full of dog treats rather than nail care equipment.

About once a month Eve comes to our house to clip and grind our guide dogs' nails. Escort is such a glutton for attention that even nail grinding is pleasurable to him. Retired Ivy lies quietly throughout the grinding procedure. Echo has not yet learned to tolerate the grinder, but willingly accepts nail clipping and filing.

Our dogs love Eve and find her multi-canine scent fascinating. As a puppy raiser for Guide Dogs for the Blind and coordinator of the Fresno 4-H puppy raising program, Eve's world revolves around dogs. The Hoopes family represents a three-generation commitment to fostering the partnership between blind people and guide dogs.

Bob Hoopes married Eve knowing her animal propensities since she entered the marriage with two Great Danes, a guinea pig and a horse! After serving in the Air Force, Bob moved his family to Fresno where the Danes shared their home with the Hoopes children, Steve and Cindy.

When Cindy was twelve, the family was given a copy of Clarence Pfaffenberger's book *The New Knowledge of Dog Behavior*. The Hoopes

When the doorbell rings, Echo and Escort wait patiently until released to greet visitors. If the visitor happens to be Eve Hoopes, their delight is even greater. Sister Pauline Quinn

were fascinated by the section on puppy raising and decided to raise a puppy for Guide Dogs for the Blind. Eve thought that by taking on this project, Cindy would focus on more than rock 'n' roll records and boys as she entered her teens.

Little did Eve realize that with the arrival of Velda, the first of the seven German Shepherd puppies raised by Cindy, a lifetime link would be forged with the guide dog movement. Eve and Cindy became so involved with the 4-H puppy raising program that Eve ultimately assumed a leadership role. Although only one of Cindy's puppies graduated, the Hoopes family was not discouraged from its goal of raising quality guide dogs.

When Cindy went to college, Eve succeeded her as the Hoopes' primary puppy raiser. She assumed responsibility for a number of older puppies who, for various reasons, could not continue to be cared for by their original raisers. Many of these dogs were given up as incorrigible and Eve committed herself to their rehabilitation.

When son Steve married, he and his wife Shirley lived with Bob and Eve for a time. Shirley brought her toddlers, Jaeson and Katie, to 4-H meetings so the puppies could be socialized to baby strollers and the presence of very young children. Immersed in dogs as they grew up, Jaeson and Katie quite naturally joined 4-H and assumed the role of puppy raisers as soon as they were old enough. Shirley often quipped she didn't give Eve grandchildren, she gave her puppy raisers!

In contrast to the work of their Aunt Cindy, Jaeson and Katie have raised Labrador Retrievers exclusively and have seen nine of their twelve puppies graduate as guides. In fact, with a smile in her voice, Eve proudly relates that her grandchildren raised three of her "grandpuppies." One of the Labradors Eve raised became a brood bitch, and Katie and Jaeson fostered puppies from three successive litters.

Cindy Hoopes in her 4-H uniform poses with Olga, a career change dog, Rosel, her guide dog puppy in training and Zipper, the family's Great Dane pet.
Courtesy of Eve Hoopes

Now that Jaeson is a senior in high school, he has temporarily left the puppy raising duties to his younger sister. Since the commitment to puppy raising runs deep in the Hoopes family, Jaeson has submitted an application to resume the role of puppy raiser when he enters college. Meanwhile, Katie and Eve travel together with their current puppies, Leander and Fiesta, all over the state attending 4-H fun days and guide dog graduations. The shared interest in puppy raising has given this grandmother an exceptional opportunity to develop an extremely close relationship with her grandchildren.

Three generations of Hoopes have raised puppies for Guide Dogs for the Blind, San Rafael, California. Shown in this photo are (from left) Katie Hoopes with guide dog puppy Golda, Eve Hoopes with guide dog puppy Lynette and Jaeson Hoopes with guide dog puppy Nexus.
Courtesy of Eve Hoopes

Whenever our schedule permits, we attend the Fresno fun day organized by Eve and her group. Each county with a puppy raising program sponsors an annual fun day. The focus is on exposing the puppies to a wide range of experiences and improving the raisers' dog handling skills. For example, people dressed in firefighters' uniforms reassure puppies that uniforms are not frightening. Musicians with trombones and other instruments introduce impressionable young dogs to street sounds commonly heard in many urban areas. Dogs see mirrors and mannequins they will later encounter in guiding their blind partners through department stores.

The Fresno Far Sighted 4-H Club meets three times a month to expose puppies to real-life situations. They take their charges to malls, restaurants and bowling alleys. Dogs are taken on stairs, elevators and across heavily trafficked streets. Once a year the group of twenty raisers boards an Amtrak train to a nearby town where they spend the day at a Renaissance Fair. An additional annual event is attending the fun day on the San Rafael campus. Many families take the opportunity to make this a weekend event. In this way they can take advantage of a ferry ride to San Francisco and a bus ride to Pier 39, one of San Francisco's busiest tourist attractions.

Raising a guide dog puppy is no different from raising a well-mannered pet. Dogs need to learn house manners such as not eliminating in the house; not chewing on rugs, furniture and family possessions; not jumping on guests; not going into the garbage; not stealing food from counters and not barking unnecessarily. Crates are encouraged when raisers are not available to supervise the puppies and tie-downs are used at night to keep curious dogs from wandering around the house getting into mischief. Raisers are encouraged to teach basic obedience and introduce their charges to as many new and different situations as possible.

The 4-Hers assume an educational role when they take on the responsibility of socializing a puppy. In California, puppies in training for assistance work do not have the same access rights as working assistance dogs. Therefore, raisers must seek permission from store owners, restaurant managers and public transportation authorities before entering with their canine trainees. Carrying out their mission of educating the public as well as recruiting future raisers, Eve and her 4-Hers set up a booth at dog shows, disability expos and the county fair.

Eve is proud of the many raisers she has worked with over her almost thirty years of involvement in the program. She says it takes a very special person to devote time, effort and love in raising a well-socialized dog and then unselfishly giving up the dog for the benefit of someone else. Comparing the care of puppies with the care of babies, she believes the 4-Hers coming through the program become better and more understanding parents as a result. They learn to be aware of and care for the needs of another living being. Babies and puppies don't always sleep through the night, they get into things and demand attention at inconvenient times. Many of Eve's proteges have gone on to professional careers related to their experience as puppy raisers. One has become a veterinarian and another is an instructor/assistant at Guide Dogs for the Blind.

Eve is proud to acknowledge that involvement in raising puppies to provide independence for members of the blind community has been, and will continue to be, her family's legacy.

Chapter Five

So You Want to Be an Assistance Dog Trainer?

In our opinion, those who train the dogs are the unsung heroes of the assistance dog movement. They work long hours in a physically demanding job with rather poor financial compensation. Most entry level positions start at less than $15,000. After many years of experience, most trainers earn an annual salary of about $30,000; some make less.

Trainers are committed to their dogs and the disabled people with whom they work. Their major reward comes from seeing the blossoming of a partnership between the dogs they have trained and those dogs' human teammates.

Trainers

A common question posed by many of our *Dog World* column readers is how to become an assistance dog trainer. Responding to these letters stimulated the idea for a piece dealing with this issue. We sent questionnaires to many of the assistance dog programs to obtain answers to the questions most frequently asked by our readers. Many of those responding to our questions were familiar with guide dogs, but learned about service and hearing dogs through stories in the mass media, dog magazines and contacts in the dog training community.

Most programs require an apprenticeship ranging from a few months to three years. Before working with disabled students, apprentices participate in all aspects of dog work, from cleaning kennels and grooming to training and placement.

Rick Holden working with his class at Southeastern Guide Dogs.
Courtesy of Southeastern Guide Dogs

The challenges of training guide dogs are demonstrated by a Fidelco Guide Dog Foundation instructor under blindfold working a dog through an obstacle course. Courtesy of Fidelco

One of the most common career paths is from professional dog handler to assistance dog trainer. Some have worked with military and/or police dogs, while others have taught obedience classes and participated in AKC Obedience competition.

Rick Holden is Director of Training at Southeastern Guide Dogs. While serving in the Air Force in Vietnam, he worked with a sentry dog. Rick's mother was blind and when he left for military service, she trained with a guide dog. After discharge, Rick returned home to Florida and worked for nine years with police dogs in the sheriff's department.

From earliest childhood, Rick fantasized about training guide dogs, but was not prepared to move north to fulfill his dream. When Rick learned that a guide dog training program had been established in the state, he applied and was hired as an apprentice in 1985.

Ralph Dennard is Director of Training for the San Francisco SPCA Hearing Dog Program. He was employed in commercial carpet sales and was involved in AKC Obedience competition as an avocation. In the mid-1970s, his thoughts turned to professional dog training as a career. The opportunity to get involved with hearing dogs was great timing for him. In 1977 he saw an ad in *Front and Finish* about the American Humane Association's (AHA) newly established hearing dog program. When he contacted AHA, they referred him to the San Francisco SPCA, which was in the process of developing a similar program. The SFSPCA liked his credentials and, after moving to San Francisco, he had the privilege of creating one of the earliest hearing dog programs.

A colleague of Ralph Dennard at the SFSPCA Hearing Dog program is Martha Hoffman. Her work history includes factory work, freelance design of crystal giftware and small business entrepreneurship. Wanting to do something dog-related, she made and sold trophies, leashes and collars for the dog show trade. In 1980 Martha got involved with dog training and volunteered at obedience training classes. As she gained experience, Martha, who is hard of hearing, decided to train her pet Yorkshire Terrier to alert her to the phone by barking. She admits, "This was a bad idea and I have spent eight years trying to untrain the barking. I know better now, of course, but the little guy is too dependent to be good material for a hearing dog." In 1988, while living in the Bay area, she heard about an opening at the SFSPCA Hearing Dog Program. She writes she was delighted to

Leader Dog trainer Phil Griffin teaching the technique of door clearance to a future guide.
Courtesy of Leader Dogs for the Blind

get the job and "It seems too good to be true to be paid for messing around with dogs!"

Angie Sumpter was our only respondent who combines a full-time career as plant administrator for an oil company with part-time employment as assistance dog trainer. With twenty years experience as a dog trainer and Obedience competitor, she accepted the challenge of training a service dog for a disabled man several years ago. This quadriplegic man's determination and positive outlook stimulated Angie's desire to train dogs for other disabled people. Like many other respondents, Angie was in the right place at the right time. At a dog show, she passed a fundraising booth set up by the Austin-based Texas Hearing and Service Dogs. Angie writes, "My nephew was born deaf and I knew something about problems the deaf faced. So, working with hearing dogs appealed to me very much." She applied for a job and has been working with them ever since.

The Training Director of this Texas program, Kelly Dillen, owned and operated Texas Hearing and Service Dogs. She is also a registered veterinary technician. As a result of her reputation in the dog community, Texas Hearing and Service Dogs approached Kelly and asked her to join the staff. "Becoming an assistance dog trainer provided me with a new dog training challenge. It allowed me to select the dogs to be trained based on temperament, breed and so forth and to train for new behaviors other than competition and basic obedience." The fact that Kelly's talents as a trainer would be utilized to the fullest to help people with disabilities was a major factor in reaching her decision to take the job.

Most of our respondents grew up with pet dogs, but Valerie Foss-Brugger grew up with hearing dogs. Her mother, Martha Foss, was not deaf but was co-founder of International Hearing Dog based in Henderson, Colorado. Since its establishment in the late 1970s, Valerie watched this program grow into one of the largest in the country. She states, "I was so impressed with seeing what my mother does that I wished to follow in her footsteps. They have a very high success rate with their placements and I wanted to be a part of it." When a training position became available, Valerie left her job in sales to join International Hearing Dog. In the intervening five years, she has worked her way up to Director of Training.

Texas Hearing and Service Dog trainer Angie Sumpter teaches a Pomeranian, Gold Nugget, to alert to a knock at the door.
Courtesy of Texas Hearing and Service Dogs

An alternate route to assistance dog trainer is from the field of animal health care. Nancy Peterson grew up in New York City and got a B.A. in anthropology. When Nancy moved to San Diego, she decided to make animal health care her new career. She obtained a degree in animal health technology and has worked in this field since graduation. Nancy's love of people and animals led her into her most recent career change as apprentice at CCI Southwest Center. Before applying for this job, she had worked with a dog trainer and read extensively about dog training, behavior and psychology. Since CCI trains dogs for deaf as well as physically disabled people, she has also taken several courses in American Sign Language to enable her to communicate with her deaf students.

Another path to assistance dog training is puppy raising. As a youngster in the 4-H club, Bruce Benzler raised several puppies for Guide Dogs for the Blind, the second largest guide dog school in the United States. Through his contacts with this program, he was hired as an apprentice and has worked his way up through the organization to his current position as Executive Director.

Sarah Holbert and Karen Acree were adult puppy raisers who supervised dog training by 4-H Club members. Both are now assistance dog trainers in Kansas.

Another instructor who got his job from the ranks of adult puppy raisers is Don Muisener. After many Florida trips to visit family members, Don and his wife, June, moved there from their home in Connecticut. Don secured a job in the data processing industry in the Fort Myers area and June got a job working for the state rehabilitation agency. For Don, the last thing on his mind was a career in dogs. However, fate had different plans for the Muiseners. June had a blind secretary partnered with a guide dog. Observing this working team on a daily basis fostered tremendous respect for guide dogs. Her fate was sealed when June had the opportunity to work, while blindfolded, with a trained dog at Southeastern. She and Don were so impressed that they committed themselves to the school as puppy raisers.

They organized a puppy raising program in their county and became regional puppy raising supervisors. In this position, they visited the school once a month, a drive of one-and-a-half hours. Don frequently teased Mike Sergeant about offering him a job and jumped at the offer when it became a reality. June was able to get a transfer to a state office near the school. Don recalls coming home with a headache almost every night from his data processing job. He glowingly reports that since joining the Southeastern staff, he rarely has headaches!

Vicki Woods was a puppy raiser for CCI. She got hooked on puppy raising when the training manager of CCI's North Central Center did a demonstration for her obedience club. When an opening in the training staff occurred, the Training Manager encouraged her to apply. In the two years since joining CCI, she has been able to combine her graduate training in psychology/learning theory with her hobby of obedience training.

A number of trainers originally pursued careers in exotic and zoo animals. Nancy Nordman was the kind of kid who brought every animal home with her. Attending college in southern California, she majored in exotic animal training and management. As part of the curriculum, she handled and trained a rat, chicken, pony, deer and tiger. Her goal was to work with marine mammals. "I wanted to play with dolphins." After graduation she worked with a variety of animals at zoos in Los Angeles, California; Little Rock, Arkansas, and Lincoln, Nebraska. For a short time, she realized her dream of working with dolphins and sea lions.

Southeastern Guide Dogs trainer Don Muisener observes a blind student working with his new dog. Courtesy of Southeastern Guide Dogs

Nancy grew up with a disabled cousin and was fascinated by her pet dog's responsiveness and sensitivity to her cousin's needs. Nancy had always been intrigued by the work done by guide dogs, and was delighted to discover a guide dog school had been established in Florida. She contacted Mike Sergeant, who was interested but was in no position to hire her at that time. She kept in touch with him and was offered a job in 1985. After seven years with this program, Nancy has moved on to other horizons in the assistance dog field.

Another person with zoo experience is Allison Rubalcava, an instructor for the last five years at CCI's Southwest Center. While attending college, she volunteered at the San Diego Zoo. She explains, "I love animals, dogs especially, and thought working with them, particularly to help others, was worthwhile."

Pat Putnam left her position as a probation officer to create Okada Ltd., a hearing dog program in Fontana, Wisconsin. Pat recounts, "I researched in the early 1980s and found there were no hearing dogs in the Midwest. The fact that we have a state school for the deaf located a few miles from us made us aware of the needs of this group of people. We were also very much aware of the needs of the local animal shelter." During the past seven years Pat has extended the Okada program to include social and therapy dogs.

Another human services professional, Clark Pappas, traded in his career in teaching and counseling for a career with CCI National. Clark wanted a job working with dogs but more than that, "I wanted a job with meaning."

Mary Coolman left her job as house manager of a battered women's shelter to join the staff at CCI North Central. Mary's response to our question about why she decided to become involved with the training and placing of assistance dogs sums up the view expressed by most of our respondents: "I wanted to enjoy my work!"

High on the list of desirable qualities for effectiveness as an assistance dog trainer are patience, flexibility, initiative, assertiveness, objectivity, creativity, empathy for dogs and people and a sense of humor. Sheena Matthew, New England Assistance Dog Service (NEADS), suggests one must have the ability to problem solve with the adaptive equipment used by disabled trainees and to instill confidence in them when working their assistance dogs. Vicki Woods mentions the ability to be well organized and follow small, graduated step-by-step procedures without taking shortcuts. Other respondents recommended the need for an ability to understand the differences in breed behavior, find effective solutions to problems and work well under pressure. Ralph Dennard sums it up this way: "Assuming a person has the talent and ability, the most important quality is to really enjoy the work. This is probably true for any job,

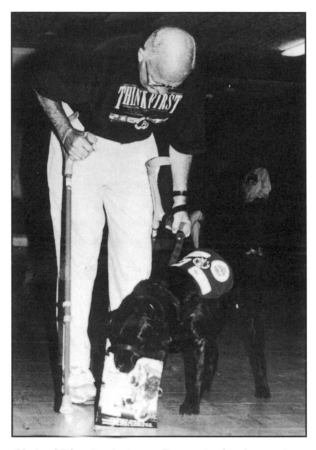

National Education Assistance Dog service dog, Star, retrieves a dropped magazine for her partner Wilson Hulley.
Courtesy of NEADS

but since there are stresses and frustrations that come with the territory, a trainer must really enjoy coming to work and working with the dogs. Someone who trains assistance dogs just to earn a living wouldn't last long or do a very good job."

Martha Hoffman, Ralph Dennard's colleague, shared with us a letter she sends to people who write to her program seeking advice about careers in the assistance dog field:

> You must be thoroughly obsessed with dogs, their mysterious and fascinating personalities. Liking animals will not enable you to hug a shelter dog soaked in urine and feces, knowing you will be dealing with more of the same all day long with no change of clothes. Many programs select animals from shelters and this is part of the job.
>
> I would say the ideal temperament for a dog trainer would not be described as loving dogs so much as being addicted to them. Things like physical discomfort, low pay and long working hours fade into the background when you feel as if any minute you may discover the magic key that lets you understand the personality of a particular dog. Dog training is like learning another language. Imagine the years of study it takes to become fluent in a foreign language so that you even dream in it. You need to learn the language of dogs, their communication by vocal and body language and be able to have a real conversation with them.

If you have a genuine desire to work in this field, but lack dog handling experience, Martha suggests:

> Train a dog. Investigate various obedience schools and find a good one. Attend every seminar you hear about. Information is available through many obedience instructors. Keeping in mind there are many different warring faiths within the field, read all the books on dog training and behavior you can get. Even if you have no interest in protection training, for instance, study it. You might learn things that apply to the field in which you are particularly interested. Earn an Obedience title. AKC or mixed breed

club titles can enhance your resume and prove that you can attain results and achieve a goal. Many people who call us do not have a dog to train at that time; borrow one.

As a child, one of my colleagues trained her dog but that wasn't enough; she went through her neighborhood and trained all the dogs she could find. There is probably someone near you who would love to have their dog go through obedience school at someone else's expense. Another alternative is to volunteer at a local shelter. It can be difficult, but you'll learn a lot. I have learned more from one dog with serious temperament or behavior problems than from twenty well-adjusted pets. In the assistance dog world, you have to know something about solving behavior problems and evaluating temperaments. Volunteer at your local obedience class. If they won't let you help out with the training classes, ask to sit and watch a few times a week. You will learn about the different dog responses to training methods. One of your main jobs as an assistance dog trainer is to communicate with the new partner of the dog about training techniques and care. It's not easy to teach people in an effective way, especially if communicating with animals has always come easier for you than for most other people. The experience in assisting at obedience classes for several years with a trainer I really admired was so important to me. I discovered you cannot just dish out information. You must communicate it so that people will understand. To do this you must understand people and really enjoy being with them.

Attend all dog shows and search out the compulsive talkers. People with years of experience in training and breeding dogs have a lot to teach you and many of them may tell you more than you will want to know. I would avoid all training schools that promise a quick education and diploma for a fee. There are some excellent schools, but check them out. In addition, no matter how good the school, it still takes years to become proficient as a trainer.

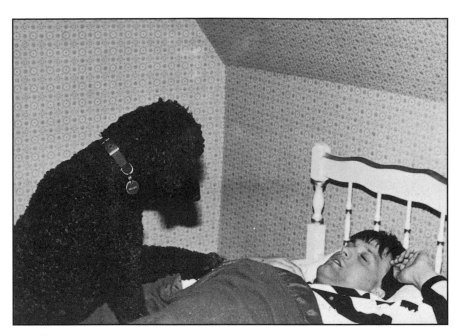

Legend, a hearing dog trainee at National Education Assistance Dog Service, alerts instructor Brian Jennings to the sound of an alarm clock.　　　　　　　　Courtesy of NEADS

Canine Companions for Independence service dog, Zambelli, opens the door for partner Becki Bushnell in order to retrieve an item of food from the refrigerator.　　　　Courtesy of CCI

Martha, like our other respondents, emphasized the rewards of working in the assistance dog field. She writes that for her, a high point is: "Rescuing dogs from shelters other people thought were trash. Some of the most amazing dogs I have met were discarded because people did not know how to deal with a dog wanting more than life as a quiet pet. It really amazes me when I see a dog matched to the right person. Suddenly the dog's and person's whole personalities and outlooks seem to blossom and the two become more than the sum of their parts."

Bo, trained by Angie Sumpter of Texas Hearing and Service Dogs, retrieves partner Toby Cole's dropped mouth stick. This device enables Toby to type, use the telephone and access other electronic devices.

Courtesy of Texas Hearing and Service Dogs

Although everyone enjoys the dog training component of the work, the overwhelming reward is witnessing the bonding of dog and disabled partner. Ralph Dennard says for him the reward is: "Knowing the deaf and hard of hearing people I work with are having their lives enriched by taking responsibility for their new dogs." Paul Mundell, of CCI, says the most rewarding part of the job is: "Seeing the placed dogs enrich the lives of those with whom they are placed and seeing how the dogs respond to this enrichment by surpassing our expectations."

For those who work with dogs rescued from shelters, the delight in observing the blossoming of a partnership between dog and disabled person is intertwined with the knowledge that a dog on death row is getting a whole new lease on life. Pat Putnam sums it up like this: "Working with unwanted, all-American mutts, seeing them come alive and bring out their special characteristics, and, above all, being able to be a part of bonding them to their special person are the rewards for me." The following story illustrates what Pat's work means to her:

San Francisco SPCA Hearing Dog Program trainer Martha Hoffman works with Dexter on responding to the smoke alarm. Deaf partners can get a good night's sleep knowing their hearing dogs will alert them in an emergency. Courtesy of SFSPCA Hearing Dog Program

I was working with a badly abused female mutt who had difficulty being touched by people. This is a must for a hearing dog, since they must make contact with their masters. At any rate, we really were not that satisfied but could see there was progress in this area. We could see the dog was working her sounds well, but touching was not easy for her. I was involved in working with her special person who was in training at the time for his two-week in-house education. Our training facility has windows in the training doors to allow us to train more efficiently. We tend to train around the clock and sounds go off twenty-four hours a day. I was up early that day and was prepared to pump a sound trying to catch the dog and her person unaware. When I happened to look through the training window, there, sitting on the chair, with his back to me, his arms open wide facing his dog, was our client. Without any hesitation, ears held erect and tail wagging, was our dog, who without any hesitation and a spring in her step, literally glided into his waiting arms. From that day forward there was no evidence this little lady had ever been fearful of a person's contact. For me, that is what assistance programs are all about. Everyone wins—the client, the dog and certainly those of us who have chosen and are fortunate enough to be part of this profession."

A San Francisco SPCA hearing dog trainee being rewarded for alerting to the telephone. Courtesy of SFSPCA

Programs that breed and place dogs in puppy raising homes have a different focus. Allison Rubalcava describes her rewards thus: "Having the opportunity to bring a dog from eight weeks of age as a clean slate and seeing the same dog graduate as a canine companion two years later. Then, seeing a team I helped bring together, and in that scene capturing the essence of what a working team should be." She enjoys interacting with the variety of volunteers, particularly the puppy raisers, who work closely with the staff and enrich the program.

Don Muisener brings the perspective of a former puppy raiser to his position as trainer. For Don, the most rewarding part of the job is working with students. He maintains close ties with several graduates and keeps in touch with the blind person partnered with the first puppy he raised.

Several respondents spoke glowingly about the impact the dogs they trained had on the lives of their disabled partners. Ellen Torop, of CCI, derives great pleasure when hearing from graduates about tasks their dogs perform that make a positive change in their lives. For instance, breaking social barriers and giving the disabled partner the confidence to venture out in public without the assistance of another person is one such experience. Angie Sumpter expresses similar feelings. She is thrilled when graduates share their experiences describing how their dogs add fullness to their lives. One graduate told Angie her hearing dog saved her life by insisting she go outside when the smoke alarm went off. Toby, another graduate, wrote about his newfound sense of independence with his service dog, Bo. Toby's father is no longer on full-time duty as an attendant. Bo will turn lights on and off and will even turn on the fan at night. On one occasion, Bo ran downstairs to alert an attendant to his partner's illness.

Ralph Dennard shares the following: "One of the nicest experiences is being told by the daughter of an eighty-six-year-old widower that her dad's hearing dog was the reason her dad had lived another ten years. After his wife died, her father became depressed and withdrawn. After receiving his hearing dog, he saw a new reason to live."

Like all jobs, there is a downside to assistance dog training. Most upsetting to Ralph Dennard is knowing some graduates have great dogs, but do not take advantage of the special qualities and abilities of their canine partners. Martha Hoffman discusses some other negatives: "Most upsetting are the dogs you leave behind at the shelters. Adopting a dog that turns out to have a fatal disease. Investing months of training in a dog that has a bad temperament and ends up biting someone. A dog you loved and trained and placed gets run over or dies of cancer. A dog is returned because it was inappropriately matched. A graduate you got to know ends up in a nursing home and the dog comes back to us. The list is endless. But unlike a lot of jobs that involve heartbreak and stress, the rewards are equally intense, maybe more intense, and never boring."

Valerie Foss-Brugger affirms Martha's feelings. She says:

> Placing and training hearing dogs is a series of highs and lows, laughter and tears. When we place a dog with a deaf person or family, it is very hard work and each one is equally as hard. It's almost the equivalent of training an obedience dog for a Utility degree. After it's finally finished, it's unreal the high you get for making this all work out. The laughter and tears you see on your recipients' faces when they come to you and tell you, 'I didn't have to worry about fire or my baby crying. My hearing dog was listening for me last night.'

Working with disabled students is like working in any obedience setting. Many people have never owned trained dogs before getting their assistance dogs and do not understand dog behavior. Sheena Matthew tells of one student who was not using his voice effectively to control his dog. She reiterated the importance of being the alpha dog and suggested he growl his commands. He took her literally and growled at his dog. "I started to laugh and could not stop. I had the whole room giggling; it was the end of a long week."

The following anecdotes reveal the lighter side of assistance dog training. While testing potential hearing dogs in a shelter setting, Martha Hoffman relates a story about a wonderful, shaggy Terrier mix, who was alert and intelligent: "I couldn't believe my luck. Attentive, friendly, food motivated, not nippy, the right age, not afraid of the pop-up umbrella or toy wind-up dog we use for shyness and curiosity. I was just about to sign the papers to adopt her when I noticed her ears were not moving and she seemed to ignore me when facing away. She was deaf! Nowadays, I test for sounds by not letting the dog see the sound producing object first. This pup was working on visual cues and curiosity. Luckily, someone was interested in adopting her because I started to have wild thoughts of training her to alert someone to flashing lights."

Angie Sumpter was training Bo, a Golden Retriever, as a service dog for Toby, a quadriplegic man. Since Toby had no muscle control, Bo was being trained to gently replace Toby's arm when it slipped off his wheelchair. Angie realized how well Bo had mastered this task when another less-disciplined Golden, in her enthusiasm to greet Toby, butted his arm off the chair. Without a command Bo rushed to reposition it.

Kelly Dillen tells the following story: "During a visit to church, our graduate and his hearing dog approached the altar to partake in communion. The dog was placed on a Down Stay on the steps leading to the altar. As the minister moved to our graduate, the dog lifted his head and stuck it under the minister's robe while still in the stay position. The congregation unsuccessfully tried to control their giggling. Despite this indiscretion, the team continues to attend services and is warmly received by the congregation."

Martha Hoffman tells the story of the hearing dog who finally won permission to attend work only to back up to the big boss' leg and have a bowel movement on his shoe. The boss' comment was: "I've been dumped on for twenty years in this career, but I never really knew what it meant till now."

Chapter Six

Award-Winning Canine Partners

Since the days of Lassie and Rin Tin Tin, canine heroes have been portrayed in movies, television, magazines and newspapers. Some of these heroic dogs save their human partners' lives by pulling them out of streams, fires or collapsed buildings. Others bring help to their stranded or endangered humans. Still others warn of fires, earthquakes, floods, or other natural or man-made calamities. Although we thrill to the feats of these superdogs, the drama involved in the everyday working relationship between assistance dog and disabled partner has a drama of its own.

Guide, hearing and service dogs, in the daily performance of their assistive tasks, provide their partners with a means of maintaining and enhancing an independent lifestyle. Sometimes these chores do take on a heroic quality that surpasses everyday events. Those rare occasions when a guide dog pulls the blind partner from the path of an out-of-control car, the hearing dog alerts the deaf person to a smoldering fire in the house or the service dog brings the portable phone to the physically disabled partner who has fallen out of the wheelchair are the stories that make headline news. However, it is the daily task of guiding a blind person through a crowd, alerting the deaf person to the ringing telephone and picking up an item dropped by a partner in a wheelchair that is the substance of the working relationship.

The Delta Society, established to foster and celebrate the human/companion animal bond, has been honoring outstanding assistance dogs for several years. We have attended some of these ceremonies and have written about the award winners. This culminated in 1993 when Toni's guide Ivy was recognized as guide dog of the year.

Applicants for the Delta awards are nominated by their disabled partners or by the organizations training them. A detailed nominating letter must be supported by the dog's trainer, veterinarian and others familiar with his/her special qualities.

Gallery of Winners

1989

As we were checking into the Parsippany, New Jersey, Hilton to attend the 1989 Delta Society annual conference, we heard the announcement that the blessing of the animals would take place in five minutes. Someone in the lobby mentioned a horse would be part of the blessing ceremony. We were excited about our first Delta Society meeting, but a horse in the lobby of a fancy hotel exceeded all our expectations!

Mary Hook enjoys a day in the country with Nemo, the 1989 Delta Society's Guide Dog of the Year award winner.
Courtesy of Fidelco

Our fantasy was shattered when we discovered the ceremony was held outdoors. Tears filled our eyes as we listened to representatives of the three major faiths bestowing their blessings on the twenty-five assistance animals present. Ivy was with us, but Ed was without a partner since Perrier had been euthanized a week earlier. For us, the high point of the conference was the awards luncheon where plaques and monetary prizes were presented to the chosen assistance dog teams.

The Guide Dog of the Year award went to Nemo, a German Shepherd Dog bred and trained by the Fidelco Guide Dog Foundation of Bloomfield, Connecticut. Nemo spent the first year of his life with a foster family where he was socialized and trained in basic obedience. His next six months of training involved riding all forms of public transportation and working in rural, urban and suburban settings. In 1985 he was teamed with Mary Hook, a twenty-one-year-old

Michael Patrick O'Shannon and service dog Barney put their heads together. Barney was the 1989 Delta Society's Service Dog of the Year.
Courtesy of Delta Society

woman who had lost her vision as a result of diabetes. Nemo guides her to work, medical appointments, shopping and the many schools and Brownie troops where she gives talks about Fidelco.

In 1987, Mary had a kidney transplant and was worried about the possibility of rejection and her need to return to dialysis. At her moments of greatest despondency, Mary would reach over her hospital bed to gather courage from Nemo's presence. Nemo had permission to stay with her in the hospital and Mary gathered strength from the desire to return to Nemo and the independence he bestowed on her.

Barney, a six-year-old Belgian Malinois slated for euthanasia, was rescued from a shelter and trained by Happy Canine Helpers of Johnstown, Ohio. He was honored as Service Dog of the Year for his loyal teamwork with Michael Patrick O'Shannon, a CPA and instructor at Ohio State University. Michael Patrick's life was drastically altered when a drunk driver rammed his car, killing his wife and child and leaving him a quadriplegic. Despondent and without hope, his life took a positive turn when Barney entered it. Michael Patrick says: "Barney is my legs, hands, protector and companion. He inspires me to go places and enjoy life. Truthfully, I do not think Barney is a dog; he just looks like one."

Robert Barwick and 1989 Delta Society Hearing Dog of the Year award winner, Rerun, do the weekly marketing. If someone calls Robert's name, Rerun will make the alert.

Courtesy of Delta Society

As a service dog, Barney carries in the morning paper, meets the mail carrier and brings in the mail, picks up his bowl when it is time to be fed, retrieves dropped items as small as a dime, enters the house first to turn on the lights at night, assists Michael Patrick in transferring from his wheelchair and pulls the wheelchair when needed.

In addition to his teaching duties, Michael Patrick acts as advisor to disabled students. He is the founder of the Ohio Wheelchair Athletic Association Swim Team. He has won numerous gold medals in national and international swim meets. Barney has been specially trained to rescue his partner from a body of water if an emergency arises.

One day when Michael Patrick collapsed from ruptured ulcers, Barney, responding to Michael's command, retrieved the cordless telephone. Dialing the emergency number, Michael Patrick explained his plight, asked for assistance and informed the dispatcher his dog would open the door. The incredulity of the medics vanished when they met Barney at the front door!

Rerun, an Old English Sheepdog mix, was the 1989 Hearing Dog of the Year winner. She was rescued from the pound one hour before scheduled euthanasia. Robert Barwick, a deaf college graduate, was employed by the Buttke Dairy Farm of Randleman, North Carolina, to manage a large herd of cows. He was frequently late for work because he could not hear his alarm clock. In addition, Robert could not hear his name being called, was occasionally in danger from farm equipment he could not hear and, on one occasion, a kicking cow got close enough to break his jaw. Robert's employer sought help from the New England Assistance Dog Service of West Boylston, Massachusetts. Due to the nature of Robert's work, it was felt a large dog was needed. Fortunately for Rerun, there were no large dogs in training at the time. Her rescue from the pound and her chance to pursue a new career led the organization to christen her with the fitting name, Rerun.

Rerun learned basic obedience and how to alert her partner to the sound of a ringing alarm clock, telephone, doorbell and screeching smoke alarm. Since Robert spent half his working day on horseback, Rerun was taught to heel next to a horse. She was trained to let him know when cows or farm machinery approached and to respond when someone called, "Robert."

Robert says: "I had been trying to hide from deafness. Now I know I don't have to have a wall around me. Rerun was the destruction of that wall."

After three extremely moving speeches, the emotions evoked in the audience were palpable. Several dogs in attendance, sensing the heightened tension, began to bark. It was apparent to all that these three award-winning animals were far more than working partners. They were loyal friends and companions, as well.

This theme of devoted companionship was reiterated the next evening at the banquet. Victoria Doroshenko and her five-year-old male Golden Retriever, Harley, received the Gil Glass Human/Animal

Bond Award. Harley was rescued from the humane society at age three by the Prison Pet Partnership Program at the Washington Women's Correctional Facility in Gig Harbor. Sue Miller, a prisoner, was responsible for training Harley in obedience and for service work.

When she was nineteen, the car driven by Victoria was hit by a drunk driver. As a result, she was left mobility impaired and subject to frequent debilitating seizures. In addition to the usual activities of a service dog, Harley alerts Victoria to the onset of a seizure. Harley senses changes taking place in his partner's body and warns her of an approaching grand mal episode by blocking her, pacing and, if necessary, barking to get her attention. As a result of this early warning system, she has the opportunity to sit or lie down, thus avoiding potential injury. Harley will then alert Victoria's attendant to the situation.

She contrasts the three years before Harley with the last two years with him, by noting the love, companionship and independence he has given her.

In all these stories, the theme of partnership, companionship, teamwork and love emerges. One striking thought is that three winning assistance dogs would have been euthanized but for the luck of being discovered, rescued and given a second chance for life through a new career. A devastatingly stark reality which also emerges is that two of the human award recipients would never have become disabled if not for the wanton stupidity of people who get behind the wheels of cars while intoxicated.

1990

As we traveled to Houston, Texas, to attend our second Delta Society conference, we looked forward to renewing last year's friendships and making new ones. The 1989 conference had been a bittersweet experience. Ed had just euthanized Perrier, and Ivy had the added responsibility of guiding us both. Ed's sense of loss was heightened by the presence of many disabled people with their canine partners. This year, he could share his joy in his successor dog, Kirby.

Once again, the Jingles awards were the highlight of the conference for us. Master of Ceremonies Bill Balaban, a retired movie director and producer, introduced the winners with a moving acclamation of the role of dogs in our lives. He said, "One word I might use to express the virtue found in the Jingles award winners is class: C—companionship; l—loyalty; a—acceptance; s—service; and, s—security."

Fiesta, a yellow Labrador Retriever, lives up to her name by celebrating life in every way. A graduate of Guide Dogs for the Blind, San Rafael, California, Fiesta was named Guide Dog of the Year. Partnered with Elizabeth Rene, an assistant city attorney in Seattle, Washington, Fiesta is an accepted part of courthouse life. Many a dour, taciturn judge has been noticed crawling under a courtroom table in order to pet her. Over dinner the night before the award ceremony, Elizabeth shared a favorite Fiesta story with us. On one occasion, this normally outgoing, friendly guide dog growled at a prisoner on his way to the front of the courtroom for sentencing. After hearing the judge pronounce the maximum sentence for this criminal, Elizabeth chuckled at the realization that the judge and Fiesta agreed on this felon's moral character!

Elizabeth and Fiesta attend church together, visit hospitals and prisons and present programs to school children. In the social arena, Fiesta accompanies Elizabeth to movies, concerts and restaurants and even has her own guest water bowl in one of Seattle's finest eateries. For Elizabeth, and the many people whose lives have been touched by this loving Labrador, Fiesta is a pipeline to the spiritual side of life.

Attorney Elizabeth Rene and Fiesta, the 1990 Delta Society Guide Dog of the Year award winner.
Courtesy of the Delta Society

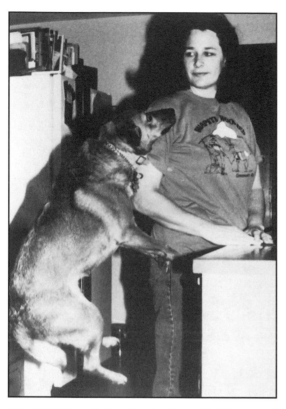

The 1990 Delta Society Hearing Dog of the Year award winner, Anna, alerts partner Barbara Biggs that the oven timer has gone off. Courtesy of the Delta Society

According to Barbara Biggs, a deaf housewife and mother of three daughters from Selah, Washington, the most distinctive feature of her hearing dog is Anna's ears. At the age of fifteen months, this Australian Cattle Dog–Labrador mix was rescued from an animal shelter and trained by Dogs for the Deaf of Central Point, Oregon. Anna, Delta's hearing dog of the year, was described by Barbara as her family's emotional barometer. If a family member is sad, irritable or elated, these emotions are reflected in Anna's demeanor.

Anna assists her partner in many ways besides alerting her to sounds in her environment. With one friendly wag of her tail, Anna crumbled Barbara's emotional Berlin Wall against the hearing world. "Because Anna goes everywhere with me, I have had to explain her presence to security guards in hospitals and department stores, to restaurant managers, supermarket employees, librarians, teachers and curious onlookers."

Anna takes her job seriously and is always on the alert for sounds her partner cannot hear. Barbara fondly calls her "Anna-ticipation!"

"She's the best dog in the world because she makes me feel different in a wonderful, wonderful way." These words were spoken by nine-year-old Travis Stout, a wheelchair user from Marathon, Florida, about Kosmic, his yellow Labrador retriever trained by Canine Companions for Independence, Orlando, Florida. This fourth grader required the assistance of a full-time teaching aide until Kosmic bounded into his life and gave him the independence and confidence we all need for personal growth. Rather than feeling left out, Travis knows he is envied by his classmates because he gets to bring Kosmic to school.

This clever service dog fetches Travis' lunch box, carries papers to the teacher, retrieves dropped items and helps Travis regain his balance when he falls. She has also given Travis' mother Kay the freedom to just enjoy having a remarkable son. With the freedom and security provided by Kosmic, Travis has adopted the motto, "I can do it myself!" Travis now believes in himself and has faith in his ability to conquer any new challenge. Travis agreed with the judges' selection of his best friend and companion as Service Dog of the Year.

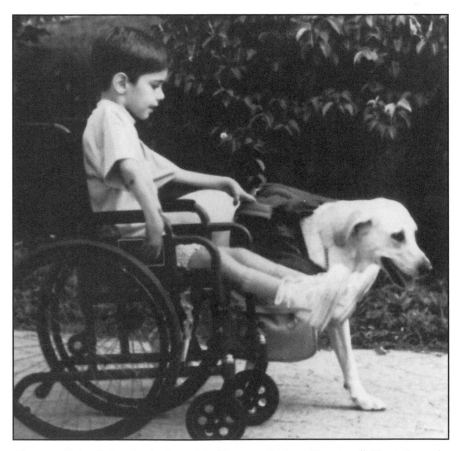

The 1990 Delta Society Service Dog of the Year award winner Kosmic pulls Travis Stout, the only child partner of a winning dog, in his wheelchair. Courtesy of CCI

Here, drawing on his training and his Labrador Retriever heritage, Kosmic assists Travis by mouth-delivering a completed homework assignment to Travis's teacher. Courtesy of CCI

Another CCI service dog named Yarrow (and nicknamed Son), trained at the Santa Rosa, California center, was honored the following day. This Golden Retriever and his partner Richard Herrin were the recipients of the Human/Animal Bond Award sponsored by Hills Pet Products and philanthropist, Gil Glass. Richard has authored a booklet, "Will You Help Me Keep My Hands Working?" which explains how Son works with him. For Richard, who has cerebral palsy and uses a wheelchair, Son is his legs, hands and feet. In an emotional speech describing what Son means to him, Richard shared with the audience his practice of keeping Son's flea and tick shampoo next to his own bottle of shampoo in the shower. "After all," he said, "Son is an extension of my body!"

1991

In October we flew to Medford, Oregon. Dogs for the Deaf was hosting a two-day seminar conducted by John Rogerson, an internationally respected British dog trainer and behaviorist. After this seminar, we went on to the Delta Society conference in Portland. As usual, we particularly enjoyed meeting and interviewing the award winners.

Duke, a five-year-old German Shepherd Dog (GSD) bred, raised and trained by The Seeing Eye™, was the Guide Dog of the Year. Duke's partner, Mike Moran of Kearny, is a rehabilitation counselor and coordinator for the New Jersey Coalition on Disabilities, Alcoholism and Drug Abuse. He also teaches in the sociology department at Jersey City State College. Adding to this rather hectic work schedule, Mike also does freelance voice-overs for radio and television shows.

Mike, blind from birth, trained with his first guide dog, a German Shepherd named Rick, in 1968 when he was twenty-two years old. Traveling with Rick opened new worlds for him and permitted him to fulfill long-held dreams. After a partnership of nine-and-one-half years, Mike was faced with the awful necessity of euthanizing Rick. He referred to the period between dogs as a time of sheer agony.

Pax, his second GSD guide, had a fullback mentality. He charged through life with his head down, and together Mike and Pax were hell on wheels. For nine years they shared a closely bonded relationship. Like those of us who outlive our beloved pets and animal partners, Mike had to eventually face the necessity of euthanizing Pax.

*Mike Moran maintains a busy schedule with the aid of Duke,
the 1991 Delta Society Guide Dog of the Year award winner.*
Courtesy of The Seeing Eye™

Mike returned to The Seeing Eye™ for the third time and was partnered with Duke. However, he was so closely bonded to Pax that during the early phase of training with Duke, he felt unfaithful to the memory of his former guide. Identifying with Mike's flood of emotion as he spoke about the loss of Pax and the difficult transition to a successor dog, Ed relived the loss of Perrier and his adjustment to Kirby.

In our interview with Mike, as well as in his speech accepting the Jingles award, he eloquently described the impact Duke has had on his life. Duke and Mike have forged their interdependence on duty, responsibility and love. Mike's partnership with Duke allows him to function at a high level of energy and accomplishment. We were impressed with Mike's dynamic, gregarious, take-charge personality. Mike believes partnership with an assistance animal empowers him and other disabled people to cope with the stress of daily living. It also provides the means for getting in touch with our own emotional reality.

Duke and Mike have become media personalities. They appeared on Sesame Street to give children a greater understanding of blindness and guide dogs. They were also selected for an educational video called "A Day in the Life of a Seeing Eye Dog." In the course of an average day, Mike and Duke might travel into New York City where they deal with noise, crowds and busy street crossings. They frequently ride trains, subways and buses before returning home to collapse at the end of the day. The confidence engendered by working with Duke empowers Mike to try unfamiliar routes and symbolizes his approach to other areas of life.

Mike briefly touched on the issue of public access, a theme that permeated the acceptance speeches of most of the award winners. He stressed the need for all disabled people to maintain their dignity by fighting discrimination and upholding the right to be accompanied by their canine partners.

Like other guide dogs, Duke is a natural social icebreaker. The most significant example of this talent came when Mike met Lynne, the woman who would eventually become his bride! Duke now has a mom and shares his home with another German Shepherd and two West Highland White Terriers. Tears came to Toni's eyes when Mike concluded his speech with a quote from a letter Lynne wrote to the nominating committee: "Is Duke a hero? I don't know, but he

Randy Moering and 1991 Delta Society Hearing Dog of the Year award winner Kim. Courtesy of the Delta Society

certainly is a dog who takes his job seriously. Each night, when my husband arrives home safely, I thank God for Duke and I thank Duke for doing a good job."

Randy Moering and six-year-old Kim of Delavan, Wisconsin, winners of the Hearing Dog of the Year award, had been together since 1987. As the result of an accident in 1984, Randy's hearing deteriorated to the point of almost total deafness. Randy also suffers from chronic back pain for which he has undergone several surgeries. As a result of his increasing deafness and a high level of medication, he was having trouble keeping medical appointments because he could not hear his alarm clock.

Randy decided to get a hearing dog primarily to alert him to the sound of his alarm clock. It was not until he was teamed with Kim that he realized how much more a well-trained dog could do for him.

Randy spent two weeks in training with Kim at Okada Ltd., in Fontana, Wisconsin. Kim, a medium-size all-American dog of mixed heritage, was abused and ultimately abandoned before being rescued and trained for eight months by Okada.

With her unusually deep sensitivity and gentleness, Kim makes an ideal partner for Randy. Kim is attentive, watches him and rarely strays from his side. Randy describes Kim as ever patient with his quirks and faults, always thinking the best about him and filled with unconditional love.

Kim boosts his morale in times of sickness or distress. During one of Randy's hospital stays, psychologists and nurses noted Kim gave Randy the strength to confront his feelings and aided in his therapy. With Kim by his side, Randy now finds people more considerate of his communication needs. Some will even take the time to write their thoughts for him to read.

Kim has made the world of sound visual for her deaf partner. This was brought home to Randy one day when Kim jerked him backwards and out of the path of a falling tree limb. Shock waves shook his feet and, when he looked up, he saw a man high in a tree wearing goggles wielding a chain saw, preparing to cut another limb from the tree. When he looked down, he saw a large limb embedded in the ground directly in front of him!

Kim and Randy moved to Washington, D.C., last January to attend Gallaudet University. College officials would not let them move into the dormitory, nor would local landlords providing housing accommodations to students rent to them. So they ended up sleeping in the back of Randy's car. One February morning, a chunk of cement was thrown through the car window and hit Kim between the eyes. Responding to Kim's persistent attempts to rouse him, Randy awoke to the sight of snow blowing in through the broken window, glass covering both of them and Kim bleeding profusely. Obviously, someone out there did not like dogs and thought animals were expendable. Randy drove to a nearby motel where he spent the rest of the night removing glass from Kim's wound. In their shared pain and fear, they both cried.

As word of his difficulties spread and he consulted with the Washington, D.C., office of civil rights, officials at Gallaudet decided to cooperate. They helped him find housing and withdrew their opposition to Kim's presence on campus. Shortly after, Gallaudet's Board voted formally to extend access rights to hearing dogs.

Randy, a soft-spoken and mild-mannered man, has taken on the role of advocate for Kim's rights and for the rights of other Gallaudet students choosing partnership with hearing dogs. In addition, he wants the deaf community to understand the incredible benefits of sharing life with a hearing dog.

Randy compared the attitude some deaf people have toward hearing dogs with the attitude they used to have toward sign language. Many felt it made them more noticeably handicapped. It is his hope that, in the future, deaf people who respect and take pride in their sign language will take as much pride in their canine partners.

The Jingles Awards ceremony is always an intense emotional experience, but when Debbie Angel, of Golden, Colorado, spoke, even the dogs cried. Debbie, born with cerebral palsy, has severe physical problems and a speech impairment. She was treated as an object of pity. Because of her unsteady gait and poor balance, people avoided her, thinking she was drunk or stupid. Another consequence of her poor mobility was frequent falls necessitating visits to the doctor.

Debbie's life entered a new and radically different phase when she met Emily. This two-year-old Otterhound, trained by Freedom Service Dogs of Lakewood, Colorado, was the Service Dog of the Year winner.

Emily acts as a support for Debbie, helps prevent her from falling and, if she does, helps her regain her balance. Debbie, who did not walk until she was thirteen, said Emily can do many of the things she, herself, cannot do. "I love to see her run, because I can feel the freedom she feels and it's like I'm running myself. When she walks beside me, I hear the sound of her footsteps and it makes me feel very strong because I know she isn't going to let me fall and hurt myself." At one point in her life, Debbie's balance was so bad her doctor wanted her to use a wheelchair. Sharing her delightful sense of humor with the audience, she told us her doctor was mad at Emily for proving him wrong!

Emily has ended Debbie's social isolation by shifting attention away from her disability. When people approach to meet her unusual-looking dog, this warm and vibrant woman takes the opportunity

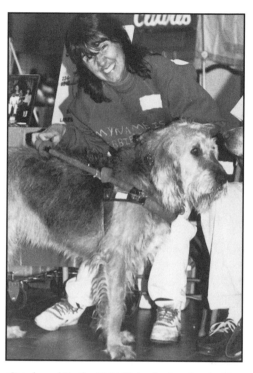

Otterhound Emily, 1991 Delta Society Service Dog of the Year, with partner Debbie Angel.
Courtesy of the Delta Society

to engage them in conversation. They learn she is an intelligent, interesting person. She is a college graduate one course short of a master's degree in psychology. Debbie is the mother of two and a part-time employee. Her husband Ray is blind and partnered with Blocker, a yellow Labrador from Guide Dogs for the Blind.

The team of Debbie and Emily, lovingly shortened to Debbily by friends, has become an energetic spokesteam promoting acceptance of disabled people and the benefits of assistance dogs. They take their message into schools and into the community.

Debbie's gratitude to her canine partner for enriching her life spilled over in her acceptance speech. Like every mother, Debbie feared her daughter would be ashamed of her. "Just before school started, my eleven-year-old daughter had two friends stay overnight. I was so scared that she would be laughed at, but because of Emily, I could have had purple spots and they would not have cared!"

At the conclusion of her speech, Debbie presented a handmade plaque to P.J. Roche, Emily's trainer. P.J. read the following inscription: "To Freedom Service Dogs for saving the life of Emily and changing my life forever!" Through a veil of tears, P.J. read from Debbie's newly published book, a poem she dedicated to her father: "Daddy wished his baby girl could walk; Daddy wished his baby girl could talk; my Daddy wished that I could run and laugh and play; Daddy died not knowing his dream would come to be. Daddy, can you see me laugh? Daddy can you see me run and jump and play? Daddy, do you know that God has set me free?"

1992

This year's Delta Society meetings were held in Montreal, Canada. The Jingles awards were sponsored by the Charles Engelhard Foundation and Pro Plan pet foods. Bill Balaban did his usual superb job as MC. Bill extolled the partnership between assistance dogs and their disabled teammates. He said: "Partnership with an assistance dog is a declaration of independence. For these superb dogs, this is their life's work, their careers. This is what they really want to do; assist and love their very special person. They are best friends, companions and partners in every facet of their person's life."

Echo, a three-year-old Shetland Sheepdog–German Shepherd mix, trained at Red Acre Farm Hearing Dog Center of Stow, Massachusetts, was named Hearing Dog of the Year. Although Echo primarily works with Joan Case, she also assists Joan's deaf husband Bill. This couple from rural Weare, New Hampshire, is the parents of three hearing children. Joan takes pride that Echo has freed the children from the responsibility of letting her know when the phone or doorbell rings or the kitchen timer goes off. Since Bill often works at night, he is relieved that his wife and children are safe with this alert and energetic hearing dog. In the course of their partnership, Echo has adapted to Joan's limited vision. Echo makes sure to establish eye contact with Joan, then lead her slowly to the source of the sound.

Bill Sloan was a college student when a terrible motorcycle accident left him comatose for six months. During his rehabilitation, a therapist told him about Top Dog of Tucson, Arizona. Top Dog introduced him to O'Malley, a Golden Retriever bred and puppy-raised by Guide Dogs for the Blind. When she proved unsuitable for guide work, she was donated to Top Dog. For Bill and O'Malley, it was love at first sight.

At the beginning of training, this thirty-year-old Tucson, Arizona, resident was nervous and self-conscious. His speech difficulties inhibited him. Training O'Malley to be his service dog was his first major undertaking since the accident. They worked on obedience and specific chores she would be asked to carry

The 1992 Delta Society Hearing Dog of the Year award went to Echo, a Shetland Sheepdog-German Shepherd Dog cross, who is notifying partner Joan Case that someone is at the door.
Courtesy of the Delta Society

out to assist him. O'Malley was not daunted by Bill's speech difficulties. When a spoken command confused her, she cocked her head as if to say: "Please repeat!" As they progressed together in their training, Bill's confidence and self-esteem were eventually restored.

O'Malley loves to work and assists Bill by bringing him his shoes and socks and the portable telephone. She makes sure Bill takes his medication by bringing him his pills, a can of milk and a cup. Bill has returned to college and learned to drive a specially equipped van provided to him by the downtown Tucson Lions Club. Three-year-old O'Malley was the deserving recipient of the Service Dog of the Year award.

Bill Sloan (seated) and O'Malley, the 1992 Delta Society Service Dog of the Year award winner.   Courtesy of the Delta Society

Blaze, the 1992 Delta Society Guide Dog of the Year award winner, accompanies partner Dan Sutorus to college classes.
Courtesy of the Delta Society

Golden Retrievers dominated the circle of award winners. The Guide Dog of the Year winner was three-year-old Blaze, trained at Guide Dogs of the Desert (GDD), Palm Springs, California. Dan Sutorus, Blaze's blind partner, began training with him in November 1990, but could not take Blaze home until May 1991. After just one week, Dan had to discontinue training as a result of serious complications from an earlier kidney transplant. Following emergency surgery and a period of hospitalization and recovery, Dan was able to complete the training.

Although Dan and Blaze had been a team for only one week, Dan was strongly bonded to this large Golden. GDD recognized the significance of this bonding and kept Blaze in working condition awaiting Dan's return. Since Norco, California, Dan's hometown, is not far from the school, the partners were able to visit during Dan's recuperation.

Having conquered several major medical emergencies and being partnered with an eager, responsive guide, Dan was ready to conquer a college career. This twenty-nine-year-old student at Riverside Community College is majoring in Russian. Dan practices his language skills by teaching Blaze to respond to Russian commands. When Blaze gets bored with professorial rhetoric, he is the only student who has administrative permission to sleep through class!

1993

Since 1989, we have attended Delta Society conferences and reported on the Jingles award winners. On July 8, 1993, the phone rangand Linda Hines, executive director of the Delta Society, gave Toni the exciting news that Ivy had been selected 1993 Guide Dog of the Year. We would be flown to New York City and honored at a ceremony hosted by Annette De La Renta, wife of the internationally renowned fashion designer, Oscar de la Renta.

In her letter nominating Ivy for this award, Toni wrote in part:

> As Ivy, my Golden Retriever guide dog, approaches her eleventh birthday, I am thankful for every day we have together. As my partner, friend and guide, Ivy has participated in an incredible range of activities. She is my pride and joy and I delight in sharing my life with her.

> In our nine-and-a-half-year fulfilling partnership, Ivy has assumed many different roles. When she joined me at Kings Park Psychiatric Center, she supplemented my job as rehabilitation counselor by becoming a therapy dog for my mentally ill patients. I did not allow patients to pet Ivy while she was guiding, but those who came to my office derived great pleasure and a sense of importance from interacting with her. Ivy's enthusiastic greeting of each

patient made each feel special and loved. One of the endearing behaviors I taught Ivy was to hug on command. When asked to do so, Ivy gently puts her paws around the requester's waist and kisses his/her nose.

During the three years we worked together in New York, Ivy saved me from injury or possible death on numerous occasions. In one memorable instance, we were negotiating a huge mound of ice blocking the cross-walk. As we slid down the mound, Ivy froze and blocked me just in time to save me from a speeding car. On another occasion Ivy saved me from falling onto the subway tracks. The station was extremely crowded and noisy and a fellow passenger, either from malice or misunderstanding, told me my train was in the station. Ivy absolutely refused the forward command, since there was no train there. Responding with more than verbal praise to these dangerous situations, I never failed to hug and kiss my fantastic teammate. For Ivy, these frightening occasions were just part of her job.

After my husband Ed retired and we moved to Fresno, California, the versatile Ivy took on new challenges. Ed and I team teach courses on disability issues to graduate and undergraduate students, including veterinary students. Seeing Ivy at work or lying quietly under a desk during long class sessions gives students a perspective on the flexibility of a well-trained assistance dog. We also give many voluntary presentations to elementary and junior high schools. I speak openly and candidly about coping with blindness, while Ivy demonstrates the way in which a guide dog functions. After the formal presentations, children who are afraid of dogs are encouraged to interact with Ivy. Sensing their apprehension, she responds to them with understanding by sitting stoically, neither licking nor nuzzling them until they show signs of being more comfortable with her.

After partnership with my first guide in 1967, I recognized the benefits of a well-controlled and responsive animal.

Working on this foundation, I began working with my guide dogs in formal obedience training and competition. Although Flicka and Charm earned the AKC Companion Dog (CD) title, it was Ivy who brought home the trophies and ribbons. After qualifying in three straight trials for a CD, we began working on the exercises for the intermediate title, Companion Dog Excellent (CDX). In March 1992, Ivy became the first guide dog handled by her blind partner to earn the CDX title. Obedience training and competition has opened up a whole new world for me and has extended the bond between Ivy and me. We are not only a guide dog/blind partner team, we are also an Obedience dog/handler team. My pride and joy in Ivy's accomplishments in the Obedience ring were renewed when we competed in shows in Bermuda. Once again, Ivy earned a CD in three straight trials.

Recently our family was rocked by the devastating news that Ed's dog Kirby had bone cancer necessitating amputation of his left front leg. After Kirby returned home following the surgery, he faced three additional chemotherapy treatments. During the period of his treatment and recuperation, the amazing and versatile Ivy assumed the role of guiding Ed. Several times a week, I would stay home with Kirby while Ed and Ivy met work obligations and did chores outside the home. What impressed us was Ivy's ability to adapt her guiding techniques to our very different walking styles and needs. I am a slow walker with bad balance, while Ed walks faster and has good balance.

When Kirby was physically able to guide again, Ivy assumed the role of mentor and motivator. With Ivy guiding me and Kirby and Ed following, she has encouraged Kirby to relearn basic guiding techniques such as going up and down stairs, threading through a crowd and carefully maneuvering around tables and chairs in restaurants.

Looking back over nine-and-a-half years of wonderful partnership with my beloved Ivy, I am so thankful she has been part of my life. As a working team, we have traveled to more than twenty states, as well as to Mexico, Canada, Bermuda and Israel. She has truly been a partner in independence. Whether guiding me through the crowded streets of New York City, strolling down a country lane in Washington, Kansas, playing ball in the park or cuddling in bed in the morning, she is my devoted friend and companion. Whether competing in the Obedience ring, providing therapy for disabled children or lonely seniors, educating veterinarians or lending moral support to Kirby, she demonstrates unfailing devotion and impeccable judgment. People tell me Ivy's face is turning white and I dread the thought of losing her. We have had a full and happy life and I appreciate and treasure each day we have together.

Toni Eames out for a walk with Ivy, the 1993 Delta Society Guide Dog of the Year award winner.
Courtesy of the Delta Society

Our hometown of Fresno celebrated Ivy's selection as the Delta Society Guide Dog of the Year by featuring her achievements on all four local TV channels and in several newspaper articles. In fact, on September 16th, the day of our departure to accept the award in New York City, we were greeted at the airport by TV cameras as we walked down the corridor toward the American Airlines gate.

We spent several delightful days on Long Island visiting friends and relatives before going into Manhattan. The Delta Society had arranged limousine service into the city, and after years of uncomfortable and unpleasant taxi rides, this luxurious service was one of many highlights of our trip. Our red carpet treatment continued at the Beekman

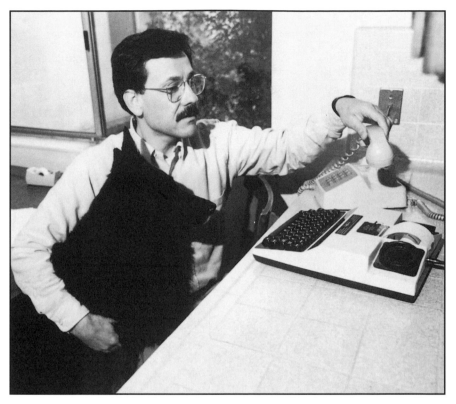

Part of Chelsea's job as a hearing dog is letting her partner Paul Ogden know the telephone is ringing. This Belgian Sheepdog was named the 1993 Delta Society Hearing Dog of the Year. Courtesy of the Delta Society

Towers Hotel where we were accomodated in a spacious, comfortable suite.

The next few days included a flurry of activity. Like famous celebrities, we orchestrated visits with friends around TV and newspaper interviews and cocktail parties honoring the award-winning dogs.

Ivy wasn't the only famous Fresno canine resident. Chelsea, a Belgian Sheepdog trained at CCI, was honored as the Hearing Dog of the Year. Paul Ogden, a professor in the department of communicative disorders at California State University, Fresno, fell in love for the second time, but his wife Annie wasn't jealous. In the early 1980s Chelsea joined the Ogden household and enhanced their professional and private lives.

Chelsea assists both Paul, deaf since birth, and Annie, hard of hearing. She is always on duty, alerting the Ogdens to significant

Joe, the 1993 Delta Society Service Dog of the Year award winner, assists partner Susan Duncan by retrieving her cane.
Courtesy of the Delta Society

sounds in the environment. Whether it's the sound of the doorbell, telephone or microwave signal, Chelsea never hesitates to bring these sounds to the attention of Paul and Annie. When the alarm clock goes off in the morning, Chelsea tries to awaken Paul. If her initial attempt is unsuccessful, she runs to the other side of the bed to try her luck with Annie.

Chelsea is a welcome sight on the campus. Whether in the classroom, Paul's office or strolling around the grounds when someone tries to get Paul's attention by calling his name, Chelsea lets him know he is wanted. Just as a guide dog learns intelligent disobedience, a hearing dog must learn when not to alert to sounds. When given the off-duty signal, Chelsea does not feel obligated to alert Paul to every ringing phone in the department.

Even before getting her award, Chelsea's fame extended well beyond Fresno. Paul's book, *Chelsea: The Story of a Signal Dog* (Little, Brown Boston 1992) describes in depth his experiences at CCI, his training of his first hearing dog and the impact of a hearing dog on his life.

On September 20th the Ogdens and Chelsea were honored at a cocktail party held at the home of Saul and Gayfryd Steinberg. Paul and Annie demonstrated Chelsea's responsiveness to both verbal and sign language commands. Demonstrating Chelsea's role as messenger, Paul gave her a note and told her to find Annie. Since they cannot get each other's attention by "calling through the walls," this messenger service enhances their lives as a deaf couple. The guests broke up in laughter when Annie read aloud Paul's note. "Please come quick. I'm out of toilet paper!"

On the following evening, Susan Duncan of Bellevue, Washington, demonstrated the prowess of Joe, a 105-pound German Shepherd cross, selected as Service Dog of the Year, a great honor for a dog handicapped with a bad start in life. Susan describes him as big and bad and formerly wreaking havoc wherever he went. Eventually, he found himself behind bars awaiting execution.

Susan, a registered nurse and mother of two, has multiple sclerosis (MS), greatly impairing her mobility and strength. Faced with the sudden death of her service dog-in-training, she visited her local humane society and rescued Joe. In exchange for his new life, Joe, with a great deal of nurturing and training, provided Susan with security and independence. MS, a progressive disease, can cause a variety of symptoms such as poor balance, lack of coordination, muscle weakness and reduced stamina, periodically accompanied by impaired vision, difficulty in speaking clearly and profound fatigue. Thus, Joe has had to master a variety of tasks and, as Susan's condition changes, must continue to acquire new skills to assist her.

With Susan holding onto his harness for balance and stability, Joe helps her negotiate stairs and, if she falls, helps her get back on her feet. When extreme fatigue necessitates using a wheelchair, Joe can be relied on to pull the chair if the battery dies. Like all service dogs, Joe enjoys a variety of retrieving chores. One of his favorites is opening the dishwasher, pulling out the racks and up-ending his metal food bowl, which he then bats across the floor. These and other clownish antics keep Susan laughing on days when her illness causes high levels of stress and frustration.

Susan's party was held at the home of Si and Victoria Newhouse. The more than 200 guests at the Newhouse home were fascinated at Joe's versatility. Susan pretended to be in bed and, when asked to do so, Joe pulled off her blanket, tugged off her socks and helped her get out of bed.

Annette de la Renta was the hostess of the party acclaiming Ivy's achievements. Among the dog-loving guests who came to greet Ivy were Nancy Kissinger and Lee Radziwill Ross. Annette's sister Sophie Craighead shared with us her incredulity that Annette lived with Terriers. Sophie proudly proclaimed her commitment to the Golden Retriever breed, which their parents had helped popularize in the 1960s.

Unlike service and hearing dogs whose skills can be demonstrated indoors, guide dogs do most of their work outside the home. However, Ivy's ability to find an empty seat and follow a designated person can be demonstrated in a home as well as a restaurant, hotel lobby or airport. As the first guide dog to achieve the AKC CDX title, a demonstration of some Obedience competition skills was essential.

Recruiting Annette and Linda Hines as auditory posts, Toni and Ivy did a flawless figure eight. Since the room was crowded with guests and precious objects, Toni demonstrated the retrieve on the flat with great trepidation. She is not known for her gentle or accurate dumbbell throwing ability! Fortunately, the throw did no damage and the guests applauded as Ivy made her retrieve.

Before taking our limousine back to the airport the next morning, we had breakfast at a nearby bagel shop. On the way to the restaurant, Ivy was jumped by a poorly behaved pet dog being walked on a long lead. Luckily, Ivy was not hurt. During breakfast we were approached by a policeman who said he saw us on the TV news the previous night. We jokingly told him we could have used his services five minutes earlier when Ivy was mugged!

In addition to local Fresno and New York coverage, CNN cable news featured the award-winning dogs. On our flight home, we were delighted and excited by the number of passengers who said they saw us on TV. For the next few days, we basked in the TV-produced limelight as friends from Canada, Bermuda and throughout the United States phoned to let us know they had seen us on CNN.

Chapter Seven

You're Never Too Young or Too Old

A frequently voiced question about assistance dogs is: "Are they beneficial for all people with disabilities?" Obviously, the answer is no. Many factors should be taken into account before recommending or deciding upon partnership with a canine assistant. However, one of the factors that does not appear to have a major detrimental impact upon working with canine assistants is age.

Although guide dog schools do not encourage the training of youngsters, many of the service dog programs are willing to train younger disabled people. At the other end of the age spectrum, all of the programs are willing to accept older applicants.

Kids

The guide dog mobility professionals are enmeshed in an age-bound tradition. Most guide dog programs not only require applicants to be sixteen, but some have recently raised the minimum age to eighteen or high school graduation.

Some reasons given are: children cannot be responsible for the care and maintenance of a dog, children are too immature to maintain the dog's training, classmates will distract the dog and disrupt the working relationship and parents will be overprotective and interfere with the dog's working tasks.

Two youngsters who debunk the myth that children are not mature and responsible enough to handle assistance dogs are thirteen-year-old Kellie Christenson and fourteen-year-old Joe Reed.

After reading a newspaper story about Top Dog, Patti Christenson of Tucson, Arizona, thought it would be a great idea for her daughter Kellie to have a service dog. Anticipating a considerable delay in bringing this dream into reality, Patti contacted local 4-H guide dog puppy raisers. To her surprise and delight, Atlee, a

After assisting Kellie Christenson down the steps of the school bus, service dog Atlee accompanies her young partner to school.
Courtesy of Tucson Citizen News—
Photograph by Gary Gaynor

two-year-old German Shepherd Dog, had just been returned to her puppy raiser after not qualifying as a guide dog. Without hesitation, the Christenson family adopted Atlee and Kellie applied to and was accepted for training with Top Dog.

As a participant in the Top Dog program, Kellie was required to attend weekly classes for eighteen to twenty-four months. In contrast to most programs, Top Dog participants train their own dogs for certification. At ten, Kellie was Top Dog's first child accepted for training. With the help of a supportive family, Kellie put in the many months of time and effort needed to make Atlee an outstanding service dog.

In the beginners class, Kellie acquired an understanding of dog behavior and worked with Atlee on basic obedience. In the advanced class, Kellie taught Atlee to retrieve on command, help her out of chairs and steady her as she steps up onto curbs. Holding the screen door open while unlocking the inner door was a problem for Kellie, so she taught Atlee to hold the screen door for her.

Before Atlee entered her life, Kellie was shy and rarely spoke to others. She brags: "Atlee has really helped me to communicate with people about my arthritis and be open about it. She's boosted my self-esteem and I feel better about myself. Now people aren't looking at me as the girl with rheumatoid arthritis, but looking at me as the girl with the dog. I know as I get older and my arthritis worsens or gets better, she'll be able to change and help me with the new things I'll have trouble with. I'm more independent because I have Atlee."

Kellie suggested that not all kids are suitable to work with an assistance dog. "You have to be pretty mature. You need patience and not give in to frustration. You have to give it your best shot and know what the dog can do for you. It can be a lot of trouble, but it's going to pay off in the end."

Joe Reed took a more traditional route to training with his service dog, Magic. Joe's mom Patti heard about Kansas Specialty Dog Service at her veterinarian's office.

In October 1991, Joe embarked on two weeks of training at KSDS. Joe was ecstatic when Magic, a thirteen-month-old Golden, was selected to be his partner. Joe is enthusiastic when describing his training at KSDS: "It was a very relaxed environment and it was real fun! I really enjoyed working in town and in the mall. The hard part

On command, service dog Magic will bring a cold can of soda to his partner, Joe Reed.
Courtesy of the Gary Reed family

was doing things over and over and over again. It was tiring and the days were very long." Patti stayed with Joe during the two-week training period and was able to observe the entire training process.

Before getting Magic, Joe, who has osteogenesis imperfecta, could not attend school on a regular basis. Joe's disease causes his bones to be very brittle and, in his short life, he has experienced more than fifty broken bones. Another consequence of the disease is extreme fatigue. Through the psychological lift and physical assistance provided by partnership with Magic, Joe now attends school full-time for the first time in his life.

Like Atlee, Magic opens doors, turns lights on and off, retrieves dropped items and carries school supplies in his backpack. Because of the nature of Joe's disability, he is sometimes unable to get out of bed. At these times, Magic is trained to get Patti. He is also trained

Magic waits for Joe's command before getting into the Reed family van.
Courtesy of the Gary Reed family

to open the refrigerator and bring Joe a can of soda. Joe's dad Gary quips that this is sometimes a problem since Magic can't tell the difference between a can of beer and a can of soda!

Joe says having Magic is the best thing that's ever happened to him. "Whenever I have a broken bone and can't get out, it's nice having a best friend who is always there to get on the bed with me or play ball whenever I want. Before I got Magic, it was very hard for me to pick up things. Sometimes, I would break a rib if I tried to lean over to grab something. Now I have a portable mouth!"

Partnership with Magic has catapulted Joe into the adult role of educator and advocate. "Sometimes it's kind of hard having him. Whenever you go into restaurants, sometimes people question you and you feel like saying, the dog is trained, just let me in and don't bother me anymore."

Like Kellie, Joe would like to see other kids benefit from partnership with service dogs. Both are staunch advocates for their respective training programs. In order to work effectively with a service dog, Joe believes a love of animals is essential. "You have to want the dog and be willing to put in a great deal of time to make the relationship work."

Patti Reed says, "As a parent, you have to learn to trust the dog as much as the child does because you are putting your child's safety into a dog's hands. We haven't left Joe with grandma and gone out of town since he was two, and we couldn't have done it without Magic. Someone always had to be home with Joe in case he broke a bone. He had no way of calling for help. Now, I can go grocery shopping and do other chores because Magic can bring Joe the portable phone if he needs to call for help."

Atlee and Magic accompany their young partners to school. Recognizing the ground-breaking implications of dogs in school, authorities provided time in an assembly setting for each child to demonstrate the dog's abilities and working functions. These remarkable kids, thrust into the role of public speakers and advocates, stressed the necessity for their dogs not to be distracted while working or to be petted without permission. As part of Joe's demonstration, he had Magic retrieve and carry a Twinkie without devouring it. To those of us familiar with Goldens, this is a fantastic feat!

By educating their classmates about the importance of the working relationship, neither Kellie nor Joe has had problems with other students. Kellie and Joe remain in control and determine when Atlee and Magic may be petted. Permission is usually granted before class starts, when they are seated at their desks and the dogs are lying quietly at their feet. Both kids report they do not experience problems in the cafeteria. Classmates respect and abide by their no feeding rules.

After a long work day at school, Atlee and Magic, remaining under the control of their young partners, unwind and become family pets. Atlee gets to play with Kellie and her brother Eric. Using a lightweight raquetball, Kellie delights in a game of catch with Atlee. Magic enjoys a game of tug-of-war with the family's pet Boston Terrier. When Joe plays tennis from his wheelchair, Magic is a willing tennis caddy.

Atlee sleeps in a crate next to Kellie's bed. Atlee is a snorer and Patti teases this is good preparation for marriage. Kellie retorts: "I can call her name and she will put her head up and wake up. I can't do that to a husband!"

Magic sleeps in Joe's bed. "If he hogs the bed, I shove him over. After all, he's supposed to be working for me!"

Both Top Dog and KSDS recognize the necessity of involving the families of students in the training process, especially when those students are children. The whole Christenson family was involved in making the relationship between Kellie and Atlee work. Although Patti was the one who drove Kellie and Atlee to class each week and observed the team's training progress, Jim Christenson, Kellie's dad, and her brother Eric attended classes periodically to learn more about Atlee's training and the commands she responds to. Patti Reed expressed her family's view of Magic by stating Joe was no longer an only child. She and Gary now have two sons to love and care for.

Seniors

Most people view the onset of a disabling condition as an unrelenting tragedy. However, our experience as members of the largest minority group in this country, disabled Americans, is that the response to a disabling condition can run the gamut from total withdrawal and dependence to treating disability as another challenge that can be met and dealt with. The seniors we feature have not let disability cramp their lifestyles.

Sixty-six-year-old Jean Feathers of Arvada, Colorado, has multiple sclerosis (MS). Seven years ago when she began having difficulty walking and bending, she decided to get a service dog to assist her with these limitations.

Jean and her husband had always shared their home with Poodles. In the mid-1980s when their fifteen-year-old Toy Poodles died within a year of each other, Jean began reading about service dogs partnered with physically disabled people. By chance, she tuned into a TV interview with Mike and P.J. Roche of Freedom Service Dogs Inc. Thinking her request was frivolous, she phoned and asked if they had a trained Poodle. To her delight and amazement, FSDI had a five-year-old white Standard Poodle being used as a demonstration dog.

After a vigorous game of fetch, Emma Fernald relaxes with her Border Collie hearing dog, Bel.   Courtesy of CCI

From the moment Jean met Gilda, she knew they were meant for each other. Having had Poodles for years, Jean was aware of and willing to take on responsibility for Gilda's grooming needs. Following the FSDI model, Jean and Gilda trained for several months together before graduating as a working team.

Like many other people with MS, Jean's physical abilities vary from day to day. At present, Jean does not use a wheelchair, but poor balance and an unsteady gait necessitate the use of a walking cane. Gilda acts as an additional support for Jean as she walks. Jean recounts with gratitude an occasion when Gilda saved her from falling as she began to slip on icy pavement.

Gilda is passionate about retrieving. With Jean's limited ability to bend, this penchant to pick things up on command is invaluable. Jean is also passionate about bingo. Gilda gets in on the act by retrieving the "pickles" (number coverings) and returning them to the barrel. She has her own rug in the bingo hall and is considered a mascot by the regulars.

Since her partnership with Gilda, Jean has had several confrontations with restaurant owners and store managers. A local store had a prominently displayed sign stating, "No dogs allowed." Knowing the law was on her side, Jean and Gilda entered the store to shop. The store manager insisted she leave and would not listen to her explanation of her right to be accompanied by Gilda. After returning home Jean called corporate headquarters and filed a formal complaint. The next time she went to that store, the sign had been removed and the canine and human shoppers were given the red carpet treatment! On another occasion she was asked to leave a K-Mart by an employee who was not aware of the role and rights of service dogs. This employee acknowledged the rights of blind people to be accompanied by guide dogs, but was unaware of the right of access for service and hearing dogs. Once again, Jean took on the role of educator and K-Mart now welcomes them and other assistance dogs.

Jean encourages other physically disabled seniors to seek partnership with service dogs. As a dog lover, Jean's partnership with Gilda has meant the expansion of a friendship with a cherished pet into a relationship with a genuine helpmate.

Another dog-loving advocate of assistance dog partnership is Emma Fernald of Spring Valley, California. At the age of eighty-two, Emma read a brochure about CCI and immediately applied for a dog.

She lived alone and her extreme loss of hearing made it difficult for her to hear the telephone, doorbell or smoke alarm.

Emma trained for two weeks at CCI's Rancho Santa Fe center in southern California. During the training period, she lived at a motel near the training center. Emma describes the training as very strenuous, but a lot of fun. The class worked with their dogs in restaurants, supermarkets, malls, on public transportation and even went to a basketball game.

Emma's six classmates were wheelchair users seeking partnership with service dogs. In the CCI model, all students have the opportunity to interact and work with all dogs in training for the first three days. Belvedere (Bel), a Border Collie, was a marked contrast to her larger Labrador and Golden Retriever classmates. Emma was delighted, although not surprised, when the final match was made and three-year-old Bel became her hearing dog.

Bel takes her work seriously. Emma says she has to unplug her phone before taking a bath because when the phone rings, Bel will dive into the tub to alert Emma to the sound! An impressive part of Bel's hearing dog repertoire is her ability to differentiate between cars driven by Emma's family members from those driven by others. Although members of the family who visit Emma drive three different vehicles, Bel will alert to these cars and ignore all others.

Emma is a retired postmistress of a small postal facility and has six married sons, ten grandchildren and seven great-grandchildren. Visit-ing her geographically dispersed family keeps Emma on the go. Last year, she flew to Montana, Florida and Las Vegas.

When Emma fell and broke her hip, her travels had to be curtailed. Bel was boarded with a friend during Emma's twenty-day hospitalization. We all know how comforting and therapeutic it is to have a dog around during recovery from an illness or accident. In true Border Collie fashion, Bel improvised on this theme. Noticing Emma's decided limp, Bel began hobbling around on three legs. She did this for three weeks with the exception of those times when Emma's grandchildren played ball with her. Under conditions of tennis ball retrieving, all four legs worked very well. With Emma's full recovery after a hip replacement, Bel has lost all signs of lameness!

One of the few times Emma had an access problem was when she and her sister-in-law, also hard of hearing and partnered with a Welsh Corgi hearing dog, were treated very rudely by restaurant staff in a nearby community. They were kept waiting an inordinately long time while customers who arrived later were seated before they were. They were finally seated at a table in a corner away from other diners. Emma was justifiably indignant at this shabby treatment and wrote a letter to the restaurant owner enclosing a copy of the California statute. The owner responded with an apology and coupons for free meals. Seeing herself as an advocate for the rights of all assistance dog partners, Emma recognized the need to educate the owner and restaurant staff and force a policy change.

Emma's advice to other seniors seeking partnership with assistance dogs is: "Just get your courage up, send in an application and go!"

Because of Florida's large population of retirees, Southeastern Guide Dogs has graduated several blind senior citizens. The onset of blindness in his mid-eighties did not stop Pardner Brown of St. Petersburg from applying for, and training with, a guide dog. In 1988 he was matched with a yellow Labrador named Golden, and for the next few years they were a familiar sight on the streets of their hometown. Unfortunately, recent health problems, cancer and a broken hip have prevented Pardner from being active with his dog. Pardner, a conscientious dog owner, makes sure Golden continues to get the exercise he can no longer provide. A college student takes Golden on long walks, maintaining his guide dog training by stopping at each curb. Right now, Golden provides love and companionship, but Pardner is looking forward to the day when they will be back on the streets taking their accustomed long walks.

Pardner's distinction as the oldest first-time guide dog partner at Southeastern was superseded in 1993 when eighty-nine-year-old Ed Kress of Naples graduated with Kama, a yellow Lab. Ed's vision began to deteriorate in his early eighties, leaving him with a severe sight loss. Fearing for his safety, Ed's daughter strongly recommended applying for a guide dog. After a wait of over a year, Ed went to Palmetto to train with Kama. When asked if he found the one month training period stressful, he said it was a wonderful experience. The most difficult part of the training was getting up at 6 A.M. every morning! Ed also enjoyed interacting with his nine classmates.

Unlike Jean, Emma and Pardner, Ed had not had pet dogs all his life. However, when Kama and he first met and she jumped into his lap, the bond of friendship and togetherness began.

Oldest first-time guide dog partner Ed Kress takes a walk with his partner Kama.   Courtesy of Southeastern Guide Dogs

With the intense heat during the day in Florida, Ed and Kama take their daily one-mile walks in the evening. Realizing her need for additional exercise, Ed plays fetch with Kama in the side yard of his apartment building.

Ed brags that Kama is an excellent traveling companion. They just returned from a one-month trip to Colorado to visit Ed's son. A retired purchasing agent and traffic manager for General Motors, Ed has two children, four grandchildren and two great-grandchildren.

Ed was surprised when we asked about access problems. He has never had a problem and believed everyone knew his rights were guaranteed by law.

Reminiscing on the impact Kama has had on his life, Ed says, "For seven years, after my wife's death, I was very lonely. Now, I take care of Kama and she takes care of me." What advice does Ed have for other seniors? He says it's the way you think. "You have to think young; you go day-by-day and you don't feel sorry for yourself."

The greatest barriers to coping with the onset of disability are attitudinal, not physical. As you can see from our featured seniors, physical, hearing and sight limitations did not stop them from pursuing active lifestyles. Their partnerships with canine helpers have minimized their disabilities and enhanced their ability to remain independent.

Chapter Eight

Taking Care of Our Canine Partners

For those who choose to share their lives with animals, veterinarians and the services they provide are an essential part of life. Their professional role is to maintain the health and well-being of the animal companions that make life a little nicer. For those of us partnered with assistance dogs, the veterinarian becomes the cement holding the team together. When medical crises occur, we depend

Authors Toni and Ed are greeted by Fresno American Airlines manager Dave Callahan on their return home from a lecture tour. American Airlines provided several travel grants in support of the Eames' educational efforts with veterinary students and practitioners. Karen Newcomb

upon these medical practitioners to restore our canine partners' health, and when this is not possible, to help us let go.

Like the general public, many veterinarians have scant knowledge about the functions of assistance dogs. Furthermore, they and their staff may be unfamiliar with the needs of people with disabilities who constitute an ever-increasing segment of their clientele.

Ed's loss of Perrier led to partnership with Kirby, who, as a result of amputation of his leg and subsequent rehabilitation, became a canine symbol for the millions of disabled Americans seeking the opportunity to continue their lives as workers, family members and friends. In the months before and after Kirby's initial diagnosis, our involvement with the veterinary profession greatly increased.

As we interacted with a diverse population of veterinarians, our goal to educate this profession about assistance dogs and disabled people became ever more urgent and encompassing. Thus far, we have lectured at twelve of the twenty-seven veterinary schools in this country and at several professional veterinary association meetings.

In the depths of a Midwest winter, Ed and Echo, Toni and Escort pose with The Gentle Doctor *after their presentation to the veterinary students at Iowa State University.*

Few visitors to the Eames' home could doubt the passionate and reciprocal bond between Toni and Disney.

Tragedy

The gripping strains of the musical *Les Misérables* distracted us as the van relentlessly carried us toward Santa Cruz. We held up pretty well until the words, "There's a grief that can't be spoken; there's a pain goes on and on . . . " hit us with full force. It opened the flood gates and our tears poured out. Still stunned from the news we received the previous day, we were on our way to the Santa Cruz Hospital–Veterinary Specialty Service to confirm the diagnosis of bone cancer for Kirby. It seemed inconceivable, but just three weeks earlier, we had made this same trip to confirm the diagnosis of intestinal cancer for our cat, Disney.

Disney's love affair with Toni began twelve years ago, when she adopted him as a four-week-old kitten from a New York rescue league. He had been bottle-fed, but weaned himself when he came to live with Toni and Flicka. Like most bottle-fed kittens, Disney's bonding with his family was powerful. In an attempt to socialize him, Toni took him to work on a regular basis. Although he became an excellent traveler, he never learned to accept new people in his life. When Ed came on the scene, Disney quickly adapted to Perrier, but only tolerated Ed. He also learned to co-exist with his feline housemates, Cameo and Kimmel.

Since Disney is not hostile to new dogs, he is useful in the training of assistance dog puppies. Puppies being socialized to become future guide, service and hearing dogs are brought to our home to learn proper cat etiquette. Sniffs and occasional licks are permissible, but nipping, chasing and frenetic activity are unacceptable. Smacks, hisses and snarls from the cats proved effective in controlling the most exuberant canine behavior.

Disney's fierceness is not all negative. He is fiercely passionate about Toni. He sleeps with her, usually with his paws touching some part of her body. When the alarm goes off in the morning, he throws himself into her arms, purring madly and covering her face and neck with cat kisses. He follows her into the bathroom and sits on the sink while she washes up. As she walks from room to room, he follows her, standing on her feet demanding to be picked up. If Toni does not respond immediately, he puts his paws up and meows plaintively until she gives in to his entreaties.

Disney spends many hours each day sitting in Toni's lap. When Toni cries, he makes a concerted effort to comfort her. No matter where he is in the house, he comes running, flinging himself into her arms for cuddles and hugs. His paws go around Toni's neck and he rubs his cheek against hers. Strangers who have not yet seen his capacity for rage are amazed at his devotion to her. Thriving on this intimacy, he often hugs and kisses her with the passion born of total bonding.

Toni was inconsolable when she had to leave Disney in Santa Cruz with Dr. Helen Hamilton. Toni knew no one would be able to comfort him during his week-long recuperation following surgery to remove the tumor and resection his intestines. Since the facility is a 24-hour emergency hospital, we phoned first thing in the morning and last thing at night for progress reports. Helen phoned daily to update us on medical details. Disney was progressing medically, but was virtually impossible for the staff to handle without sedation. Toward the end of his hospital stay, Toni asked Helen if Disney was one of the worst patients she ever had. After a short pause, Helen said, "No, he isn't *one* of the worst; he is *the* worst!"

Everyone celebrated when Disney was ready to come home. The hospital staff was impressed when Toni reached into the cage to pick up a raging Disney and he was immediately transformed into a clinging, loving kitty.

With the surgery and hospitalization behind us, we thought the worst was over. Little did we know, the next month was to be filled with a series of nightmares.

Several days after returning home, Disney developed a severe upper respiratory tract infection that quickly spread to the other cats. Kimmel, our youngest cat, recovered quickly, but eleven-year-old Cameo became seriously ill and she and Disney stopped eating. They required syringe feeding, subcutaneous fluids and lots of medication.

Whenever we have faced crises, we have managed to locate rescuers. In this crisis, our magic genie was Michelle Price, a veterinary technician working for our cats' veterinarian. Michelle agreed to visit twice a day to minister to our ailing feline family members until they were fully recovered. The day we took Disney home from Santa Cruz, we mentioned to Dr. Hamilton that Kirby had a minor limp. She brought him across the hall to see Dr. Darcy Palmer, an orthopedic surgeon. Darcy saw no visible cause for the limp and suggested it might be a pulled muscle.

Two weeks later Ed and Kirby returned from a trip to the East Coast where they did an extensive amount of walking. Realizing Kirby was in pain, Ed took him to Bob Larsen, our local veterinarian. Although we conjured up every conceivable scenario, we were unprepared for the devastating news. Dr. Larsen, who had examined Kirby just one week earlier, could hardly believe the results of the X rays. There was clear evidence that an aggressive tumor had destroyed most of the ulna, one of the large bones of the foreleg. Once again, we heard the dreaded word cancer and were thrown back into the depths of despair. When we asked Bob about treatment and heard the word amputation, it felt like our world was crumbling.

The next day we were on the road to Santa Cruz for a biopsy to determine the type of cancer and the course of treatment. Later that night we returned home with an anesthetically induced disoriented Kirby.

Waiting for the results of the biopsy while simultaneously deal-ing with Disney and Cameo's debilitated condition was sheer emo-tional torture. Our lives had been turned upside-down. It seemed unreal to be wishing Kirby had the "good" (less lethal) rather than the "bad" (more aggressive) cancer. The torment of waiting ended with the diagnosis of chondrosarcoma, not the best, but not the worst.

Our hopes that amputation could be avoided by limb salvage surgery were dashed when leading veterinary oncologists concurred with the recommendation for amputation. Helen consulted Dr. Steve Withro, the Colorado-based expert on limb salvage. We consulted Dr. Ann Jeglum, the Pennsylvania-based research oncologist we met several months before in Bermuda. Miracles did not happen and on February 12, 1993, we were on the road again to Santa Cruz taking our Kirby, a six-year-old guide dog and AKC Obedience competitor, for chemotherapy and subsequent amputation of his left front leg and shoulder. All the way to the hospital we struggled with the idea that we were subjecting this beautiful, happy-go-lucky Golden Retriever partner in independence to such a radical mutilation of his body. However, deep down we knew we had no other option.

With the cats still refusing to eat and the uncertainty of Kirby's future, our emotional devastation seemed unending. Although Darcy was Kirby's primary care veterinarian, both she and Helen remained in close touch with us. The hospital staff was impressed by Kirby's willingness and ability to ambulate following his surgery. In fact, he was ready to come home two days later.

Kirby's Rehabilitation

"Your dog sure is loyal!" "He certainly loves you!" "That's one brave dog!" We reveled in these words of support for Kirby, our wonder dog. When we contemplated rehabilitating Kirby as a three-legged guide, we were not sure how the public would react. Several people warned us our decision might generate public hostility. To the con-trary, statements like those quoted above demonstrated the public's support and encouragement of our efforts.

The only criticism we received was from other guide dog part-ners. These critics believed that by continuing the partnership with a disabled dog, we were demeaning the image of guide dogs and offending the sighted public. Some have extended their criticism to Guide Dogs of the Desert for their support of us.

Back in February, when Kirby was first diagnosed, we thought his career as a guide was over. Following the amputation, he was reluctant to move unless coaxed to do so. The only exception was at feeding time. We require Kirby and Ivy to maintain a Down Stay under the dining room table while their food is prepared. Ivy's bowl is put down on the floor to the right of the kitchen counter and Kirby's on the left. They wait drooling and quivering for the signal to eat. The day we brought Kirby home from the veterinary hospital, he was so lethargic we did not think he would be interested in eating. What an underestimation of his Golden Retrieverness! Ivy waited under the table, but we left Kirby stretched-out in the middle of the floor. To our amazement, at the eat signal, Kirby jumped over Ivy to get to his bowl! If we had not been so devastated at the time, we would have realized nothing would keep Kirby down for long.

Day by day, we saw marked improvement in his ability to ambulate. He no longer had to be encouraged to join us upstairs in the computer room or to go outdoors for relief. A month after the amputation Kirby had regained a great deal of strength and stamina, but still did not roll or play one of his favorite games, chasing Kimmel. Much to our delight, within a few days, we heard the familiar grunts and groans of Kirby rolling around the floor. Meanwhile, Kimmel used all of his feline wiles to induce Kirby to chase him. It was painful for us to know that Kirby was remaining motionless while Kimmel rubbed back and forth across Kirby's face and chest. About two weeks later we let out whoops of joy at the sound of our three-legged wonder dog chasing Kimmel throughout the house!

We hated leaving Kirby home during this recuperative period. When Toni harnessed Ivy, he came hopping to the front door expecting to accompany us. Never imagining he could actually guide, we took him with us one day to our favorite Chinese restaurant where the proprietor has always been delighted to see our dogs. After getting out of our friend's car, Ed picked up the harness and, to our disbelief, following Ivy's lead, Kirby guided Ed into the restaurant. This brief experience left us confused about Kirby's future.

At a lecture we presented to the veterinary students at the University of California, Davis, we received a great deal of encouragement to rehabilitate Kirby as a guide. Despite the necessity for three post-surgical chemotherapy treatments, bolstered by the veterinary students' positive outlook, we began exploring the possibility of rehabilitation.

Before making any firm decision, we consulted several surgical veterinary specialists who advised us to build Kirby's stamina and muscles by taking him for long walks and giving him the opportunity to run. Since these activities would place additional stress on his hips, we had them x-rayed, and there were no signs of dysplasia. Clearing this hurdle, we explored ways to initiate an exercise program.

We did not want to take long walks with Kirby in harness because, we believed, this would put undue pressure on him. An acquaintance suggested that her nineteen-year-old brother, Kent Phelps, might be interested in assuming the responsibility for walking Kirby. Kent was thrilled with the thought of interacting with a large dog and helping with Kirby's rehabilitation. Twice a week, Kent drove his motorbike the two miles from his home to ours. At first Kent and Kirby took short walks. Once we felt comfortable with Kent taking Kirby out, we added Ivy to the equation. As these walks increased in length and duration, Ivy, the ten-year-old, benefitted as much as three-legged Kirby. The only break in this regimen was when Kirby was hospitalized for chemotherapy treatments.

As Kirby's stamina improved, we added playtime to Kent's visits. Under his supervision, Kirby and Ivy ran, chased and retrieved a flip stick, a toy that bounces unpredictably when thrown.

It didn't take long for our fun-loving Goldens to associate Kent's arrival with a good time. At the sound of his motorbike, the dogs raced frenetically around the house in anticipation of his arrival. Ivy greeted him with a toy, while Kirby had taken to emitting high-pitched squeals of delight. Kent's bond with the dogs had grown to the point that, when his bike broke down, he walked the two miles to keep his appointment with them.

Not only has Kent been instrumental in Kirby's rehabilitation, but in a funny way, the situation has been reversed. Kirby has also helped Kent. In July, we learned there was a job opening at Dr. Larsen's office. Kent immediately came to mind and at our urging, applied for the job and was hired. Prior to this he was a part-time employee at a fast-food restaurant working for minimum wage. His new job is full-time, pays better and has the potential for redirecting his career goals. His devotion to Kirby and Ivy can now be extended to other companion animals.

Another friend who was instrumental in Kirby's rehabilitation was Pat Johnson. Pat, a busy mother of two school-age children, came twice a week to drive us to a nearby park where the dogs could run after tennis balls. Ivy also helped Kirby develop as an agile three-legged athlete. If Kirby retrieved the ball, Ivy would tackle him in the attempt to get it away from him. He quickly learned to sidestep Ivy, even spinning in tight circles to avoid her. This maneuver greatly helped him when he later guided Ed in restaurants where it was necessary to weave between tightly-packed tables and chairs.

In mid-April, with the chemo treatments behind us and Kirby reemerging as a strong, powerful dog, Ed began reasserting the partnership with him as guide. Through our consultations with numerous veterinary specialists, we knew Kirby could physically handle his guiding responsibilities. Carefully evaluating Kirby's emotional and mental state of mind, it was clear to us that he preferred his role as working partner to that of stay-at-home pet.

Kirby, a consummate tail wagger, showed no stress when working in harness. However, his guiding was less than adequate. It was obvious Kirby remembered his responsibility of guiding Ed safely around obstacles and stopping at curbs and steps, but he was extremely hesitant and frequently stopped for no apparent reason. Only after a great deal of coaxing from

Three-legged Kirby proved to the world that even for animals, disability does not mean the end of an active working life. Jerry Hensley

Ed would he resume his guide work. We attributed this hesitation to the lingering effects of his medical ordeal.

Despite our doubts, we were not going to give Kirby up as a guide without a struggle. In early June we turned to another Bermuda contact, Ian Dunbar, a renowned animal behaviorist and veterinarian. We phoned Ian at his home in Berkeley, California. He listened to our description of Kirby's pattern of behavior and suggested several explicit behavioral modifications to alleviate the problem.

Ian diagnosed the situation as learned helplessness. By feeling sorry for Kirby and always allowing Ivy to take the lead, we had unintentionally taken away his initiative. Ed compounded the problem by coaxing and cajoling Kirby when he hesitated. As Ian pointed out, Kirby had come to enjoy all the positive attention he received by not moving forward at the first command. Suggesting Ed would have to be his own guide dog during the retraining, Ian told him to carry a white cane to be used when Kirby refused the Forward command.

For his courage and loyalty, Kirby was posthumously inducted into the California Veterinary Medical Association Animal Hall of Fame. While Toni and Ivy look on, Dr. James Harris, Chairman of the CVMA Human-Animal Bond Committee and Dr. Jim Sokolowsky, representative of Waltham, sponsor of the annual award, present Ed and Jake with a plaque, a certificate for a one year supply of Waltham dog food and a check for $500.

Robert Martinus

Ian Dunbar, renowned veterinarian/animal behaviorist, was instrumental in Kirby's return to work as guide. Ed, Ian and Toni reaffirm their relationship begun several years earlier. Service Dog advocate Jean Levitt rounds out this congenial group. Brad Scott

If Kirby did not move on the first command, Ed was to drop the harness and leash and, using a white cane to safely move along the street, leave Kirby where he was. Leaving him behind would, according to Ian, deliver a clear message to Kirby. "I would rather be doing this with you, but if you won't guide me, I'll have to do it without you." Tapping into a Golden's need to be with his partner, Ian predicted this demonstration of Ed's independence would trigger Kirby's need to re-assume his role as guide and working partner. Within a few days of employing this abandonment tactic, Kirby showed phenomenal improvement in his response to the Forward command.

To add an element of surprise to the routes, as suggested by Ian, we arranged for friends to meet us at designated spots. On some walks our friend Linda Haymond greeted Kirby with a biscuit in

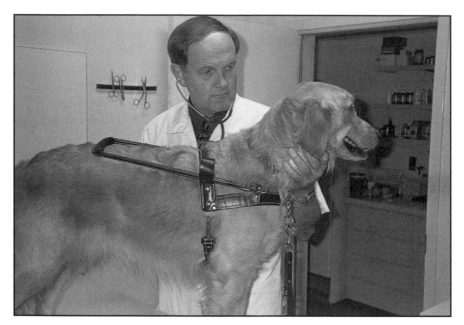

Dr. Robert Larsen examines guide dog Echo. Maintaining the health of the canine partner is the job of caring and skilled veterinarians.   Karen Newcomb

hand and gave us all a ride home. On other occasions Pat Johnson met us and the reward was a ride to the park and a game of tennis ball.

In mid-July we traveled to Berkeley to meet Ian and show off our three-legged wonder dog. Ian was impressed with Kirby's spirit, as well as his performance as guide. At the end of a demonstration walk, he brought tears to our eyes when he said, "That Kirby really has heart!"

In late April 1994 Kirby went in for his semi-annual chest X ray. We were devastated by the news that the bone cancer had metastasized to his lungs. It seemed inconceivable we might lose him. Just three weeks earlier he and Ivy were guiding us along the congested streets of Philadelphia, New York and Boston.

As the cancer spread and took its toll, Kirby's life force gradually ebbed from his body. His many friends and admirers came to the house to say their final goodbyes, providing us with loving support and the opportunity to share our intense grief. On Saturday, June 4th, Dr. Larsen came to our home to humanely end the life of this spectacular animal. Although Kirby had been Ed's guide for only four-and-one-half years, he had a tremendous impact on shaping the public's attitude toward disability. He proved to the world that even for animals, disability does not mean the end of an active working life. To honor his courage and loyalty, the California Veterinary Medical Association inducted Kirby into their Animal Hall of Fame in September 1994.

Veterinarians, Disabled Clients and Assistance Dogs

Toni sat on the floor in Dr. Jerry Tobias' examination room cradling Flicka in her arms. Tears began flowing as he broke the awful news that Flicka was terminally ill. Jerry's prognosis not only triggered the grief we all feel at the impending loss of a beloved companion, but also set in motion a myriad of other feelings. Flicka's impending death forced Toni to be practical when she would rather have wallowed in grief.

Jerry, Toni's veterinarian for fifteen years, was familiar with the duties of a guide dog. Working together, Jerry and Toni developed a treatment strategy permitting Flicka to continue working while Toni made plans for Flicka's successor. Through this experience, she gained greater insight into the essential role of veterinarians in the lives of disabled people partnered with assistance dogs. Toni's working relationship with Jerry expanded when Ed entered her life and Jerry took on the care of Perrier.

In 1987 when we moved to California, our attempts to convince Jerry to relocate in Fresno failed. We now had to search for a successor veterinarian.

Since moving to Fresno, we have been writing and lecturing about disability issues with an emphasis on assistance dogs. One aspect of this new career is exploring the relationship between veterinarians and disabled clients. In 1994 we assisted the American Veterinary Medical Association (AVMA) in the preparation of a pamphlet dealing with the special needs of elderly, chronically ill and disabled clients. In preparing this material, we explored our own experiences as well as those of our fellow assistance dog partners.

Lecturing to Fresno County veterinarians and veterinary students at the University of California at Davis and Cornell University launched us on a new career. In our work with these medical practitioners, we always emphasize the importance of understanding the specific functions of assistance dogs in order to treat them effectively. We use the following situations to illustrate this point.

Before Ed met Jerry Tobias, he brought Perrier to the Animal Medical Center in New York City to have a cyst removed from his ear. Perrier was given a general anesthetic for this procedure and was apparently over-anesthetized. A friend drove Ed and Perrier home from the hospital with instructions to rest him for the remainder of the day. The following morning Perrier was willing to work but was not able to make clear-headed decisions. While crossing a major thoroughfare, Perrier was disoriented and confused. Fortunately, a son of a colleague rescued and escorted them to Ed's office. In treating a guide dog, the veterinarian must be aware of the necessity for alertness when prescribing medication or other treatment procedures. If alternative treatment protocols are not possible, the blind person must be temporarily advised not to rely on the dog.

On another occasion, Perrier received a bad cut on his paw. Like most accidents, this occurred on a Sunday when Jerry was not available. The veterinarian at the Animal Medical Center stitched the paw but did not wrap it. We explained that Perrier was a guide dog and we had to walk six blocks from the subway to our home. Despite our explanation, the veterinarian insisted this was the correct procedure. Not unexpectedly, several stitches had come loose by the time we arrived home and an infection set in. When we got to Jerry's office Monday morning, he was appalled at the condition of the paw. He had to re-stitch the wound and with his paw properly bandaged, Perrier continued to function as a guide while the paw healed.

When Ivy and Perrier required teeth cleaning, Jerry did not anesthetize them for the procedure. He believed that with dogs who were placid and compliant, it was better to do a less thorough job more frequently than to expose guide dogs to the risks of anesthesia. Most other veterinarians we know adhere to the position that a thorough cleaning under anesthesia is necessary to maintain good health. If they understood the years of effort and training it takes to develop an effective working team, they might consider the merits of Jerry's position. Furthermore, the disabled partner is forced to relinquish the dog's services for all or most of the day of the procedure.

Shortly after we moved to Fresno, Perrier needed the care of a specialist and we took him to the University of California, Davis Veterinary Hospital, a distance of 200 miles from our home. He was diagnosed with lymphocytic gastritis and an extremely high level of prednisone was prescribed. A side effect of this medication is a continuous need to drink, leading to frequent urination.

Our Davis veterinarian, a young resident specializing in gastrointestinal problems, had little knowledge of the working role of a guide dog. He did not realize Perrier accompanied us to lectures, meetings and other functions where he had to lie quietly for several hours before being taken out for relief and flew with us in the passenger cabin when we traveled by air. Until the prednisone was reduced to a manageable level, we had to cancel all activities outside our home.

Since we are writers and itinerant educators, we could make the necessary adjustments to care for Perrier. This medical regimen would have been impossible in New York City with Ed's daily one-and-a-half hour commute each way by subway to his office located on the fifteenth floor of an office building.

Obviously, within the profession, considerable variation exists among veterinarians and veterinary hospitals regarding their knowledge about and sensitivity to the needs of disabled clients partnered with assistance dogs. Among the suggestions we made in our lectures were for veterinarians to interact directly with disabled clients and, wherever possible, be flexible in scheduling appointments. Disabled people are offended when questions and comments are not directed to them, but rather to their non-disabled drivers, interpreters or personal assistants. Many disabled people do not drive and must depend on public or para-transportation, taxis or a lift from a friend to get to their veterinarians' offices. Meeting a rigid time schedule may be difficult, if not impossible.

Clients with different disabilities have different needs. It may be necessary to write instructions for treatment and care for deaf clients who do not speech read. Blind clients may need hands-on demonstrations of treatment procedures, such as ear cleaning, administering eye drops, or changing dressings. Syringes can be notched for blind clients to indicate the amount of liquid medication needed. If more than one medication in similar containers is prescribed, some technique, such as the use of rubber bands, could be used to differentiate the containers. Since people with physical disabilities vary tremendously in their hand-motor skills, it is best to work out individual treatment plans.

Although we did not mention it in the brochure, a sensitive issue we discuss with veterinary students is fee structure. Since two-thirds of disabled Americans are unemployed or underemployed, they constitute the most impoverished segment of society. Many live on the federal Supplemental Security Income program, which provides less than $450 a month. Although veterinary care has not skyrocketed to the extent of human medical costs, it still represents a major investment for those at the lowest end of the income spectrum. Veterinary costs, combined with the cost of providing a high quality dog food, have acted as economic deterrents for many disabled people considering partnership with assistance dogs.

We spent more than $1,500 when Perrier was ill, including transportation, testing at the Davis veterinary school and several nights in a hotel while he was undergoing tests. Kirby's treatment for cancer involved an expenditure of more than $3,000. Fortunately, we could handle these expenses without bankrupting ourselves.

On the other hand, when Jessica's five-year-old guide dog needed a diagnostic work-up, Jessica could not afford the expensive testing and felt she had no option other than retiring her dog. Because of her limited income, Jessica had to break the bond with her partner of three years and retrain with a new dog. After two years of teamwork, Michelle's service dog was diagnosed with severe hip dysplasia. She could not afford the expense of hip replacement surgery and was forced to euthanize her dog. Mark's hearing dog developed chronic allergies and needed several medications to keep him comfortable and working. Mark, who was unemployed and received Supplemental Security Income, was unable to assume this additional expense and had to send his best friend back to the facility that trained him. In these cases, as well as many others, the team could have been maintained if programs existed to offset the financial burden on those least able to pay.

One approach to minimize this burden is to turn to veterinarians for assistance. While attending the American Animal Hospital Association meetings in San Francisco in 1990, we surveyed more than fifty veterinarians. Some had no assistance dog patients and therefore had no reduced fee policy. Others had policies ranging from no discount to free care with only at-cost charges for tests and medications. Between these extremes, we found discounts from ten to thirty percent and variable fees depending on the clients' ability to pay. Some university-based veterinary hospitals offer discounted treatment and the Animal Medical Center in New York City, the largest animal hospital in the country, offers free care, tests, treatment and medication to guide dogs.

It would be unfair to place the financial burden of reducing the costs of medical care for assistance dogs on the backs of veterinary practitioners, who are not the most highly paid medical professionals. We call upon the pharmaceutical companies and dog food manufacturers to help defray the costs of care for assistance dogs.

Another approach is to turn to the assistance dog providers for help. Several guide dog schools assist their graduates by providing financial assistance with veterinary bills. Some programs provide veterinary care free of charge for graduates who bring their assistance dogs to the training facility. A number of states provide assistance dog maintenance allowances for those receiving Supplemental Security Income.

One of the most ambitious, innovative and far-reaching programs developed to ease the financial burden of assistance dog partnership has been created by Kansas Specialty Dog Service (see Chapter Three). If other state veterinary medical associations would follow the example of the Kansas VMA, which has fee structure, we would anticipate a tremendous growth in the demand for assistance dogs. We would also anticipate an era in which individuals like Jessica, Michelle and Mark would not be forced to break the bond with their assistance dog partners because of economic hardship.

Chapter Nine

Breaking the Bond

Many of us who live with pets incorporate them into our lives as family members. The intensity of the pet/person relationship cannot be fathomed by those who are not "pet people." When this relationship is reinforced by the everyday working partnerships between assistance dogs and their human teammates, that intensity is even deeper. When it becomes necessary to terminate the relationship with an assistance dog for any reason, the grief felt at relinquishing the partnership is profoundly traumatic.

Despite the lethargy engendered by cancer treatment, Flicka rallied for this romp with Toni's colleague Dorothy Dengel.

Since a dog's life span is shorter than a human's, the decision to work with a canine assistant will in most cases eventually lead to the loss of the dog and the end of the partnership. Working with assistance dogs is a cycle of love and loss. Not all losses are the result of the aging process and disease. Ed's early retirement of Jake demonstrates that one grieves for a lost canine partner even if the loss is the result of the dog's inability to accept the role of guide.

Love and Loss

Several months before Ed met Toni, he read in the *Newsreel*, a cassette magazine by and for the blind, a tribute she wrote to her dying guide dog. At that time Perrier was young and healthy; the last thing Ed wanted to think about was a future in which his loss would become a reality. Unfortunately, none of us can escape the reality of illness and death.

Following the experience of a similar loss, the following words written by Toni became far more meaningful to Ed.

> I sit in my apartment watching the life fade from my faithful Flicka. I wish my love, which is so strong, so ardent, so very fierce, could save the animals I love so they would never die; never leave me alone. However, I am a realist and know Flicka would not be with me today if Charm, my first-born, most wonderful guide, had not died. I would not trade the intensity of my love for the mediocrity of indifference, but, oh how cutting and devastating is the pain of love and loss!
>
> A guide dog is a miraculous animal. Every day of her working life she devotes herself to keeping her partner safe. I remember the countless times Flicka guided me around obstacles, taking extra caution with cracks in the sidewalk, walked on the ice as slowly as a snail with arthritis because she learned to identify with my terror of falling, and the many times she stopped for moving vehicles some of which I could not hear or anticipate. She kept me safe for over six years, often subordinating her instincts to do so, and I feel helpless because I cannot reciprocate.

This damned cancer is murdering my precious, beloved Golden Retriever and I cannot keep her safe!

Friends are very important at a time like this. The pain is incredibly intense. Knowing many people care, letting me know they are in reach of a telephone or a hug, really helps. Oh, thank you, dearest friends, it helps! Flicka is so well-loved, so vital, so joyous, her pending death is a wrench and a heart-shredding pain to her many fans.

What about Dorothy's grief? She became Flicka's god-mother shortly after Flicka came into my life. Flicka adores her and, at her moments of deepest lethargy on this dreadful, life-prolonging medication, Flicka will rally for a run with Dorothy. I witness the devastating blow Flicka's illness has dealt this gentle loving woman and again, I feel so helpless!

What about my mother and my dearest friends? They stand by in the same helpless position watching us both, the dog and me, suffer. I know they would drop everything and come to me when I need them and the knowledge of their love and compassion comforts and protects me.

What about my wonderful, gentle and brilliant veterinarian? He suffers too, with the recognition that his knowledge and medical bag-of-tricks cannot stop the relentless course of this disease, this killing cancer. He sees my tormented face, my tears, my fears. He cares deeply and I love him.

I need someone to hold me tight and let me melt, suspending me above the harsh realities of living, of dying. It is so difficult to always be strong, to have fortitude, to have the patient courage to take one day at a time.

Seven years ago Flicka met Charm, my first guide dog, the day before Charm died. Did Charm actually pass on her expertise to Flicka? Is that why Flicka is such an outstanding guide? Now Flicka and newly acquired puppy Ivy are friends and travel companions. Will Flicka transmit her loyal, devoted guide dogness to Ivy? Will it comfort Flicka to know that Ivy will be able to take over when death claims her? I want so much to believe!

I promise, darling Flicka, I will not let you suffer; I will try to let go gracefully. When the time comes for our final parting, know you are adored and your memory will live forever in my mind, my heart and my ability to face the future.

September 6th, Perrier's tenth birthday, was a bittersweet day. It began like most other days with Perrier and Ivy joining us in bed at the sound of the alarm clock. This morning ritual, when the dogs joined the cats on the bed for cuddles and hugs, was pleasurable for all of us. This day was different; it was the last birthday Perrier would celebrate with us.

Like many dog owners, I fantasized that my black Labrador would live in good health to become the longest lived dog of his breed and enter the *Guinness Book of World Records*. The grim reality, however, was that Perrier had lymphocytic gastritis and this was the last celebration we would have together.

After many consultations with our local veterinarian, two visits to the University of California, Davis Veterinary Hospital, several changes of diet and a variety of drug protocols, his health continued to deteriorate.

It had become apparent to me that Perrier's declining health was having a negative impact on his effectiveness as a guide. He was nervous in crowds and was displaying noise sensitivity. One consequence of the continued use of prednisone was his need to be taken out to urinate every hour and a half. He had not had a solid bowel movement in two months. Because of the urgent need to get him out frequently, sitting through a play or lecture was difficult and traveling long distances was impossible.

I made the painful decision to apply for a new guide dog. My desire to keep Perrier as a pet was shattered by the realization of his increasing need for constant care. He could not be left alone for any length of time because of the nature of his illness and his tendency to bark nonstop when he was separated from me. I toyed with the idea of finding another home for him with someone who was home most of the day. But who would I find who would get up in the middle of the night to take him out, clean up after acute episodes of vomiting and diarrhea, prepare frequent meals of boiled rice and cottage cheese and spend large sums of money on medication and veterinary bills?

After eight years of a working partnership, I felt I owed Perrier a great deal. Apparently he was in no pain, but could not have been comfortable. He no longer played with Ivy and didn't bother to greet our friends when they visited. The quality of my life had also deteriorated. I could no longer comfortably travel with him; nor could I have peace of mind leaving him behind. As I contemplated the idea of

Flicka serves as role model for young Ivy who is in training to become Toni's new guide.

euthanasia, I felt guilty when I focused on the diminished quality of my life. If I curtailed my activities, I could have kept Perrier going for a few more months. However, I was not prepared to do this. His health would continue to decline and I needed time to devote to my new dog, which would include three to four weeks at a residential training center. Given all these considerations, I reluctantly made the decision for euthanasia.

A close friend, an animal health technician, arranged to have a veterinarian come to the house to euthanize my partner. We held Perrier and patted him as his life gently slipped away. Part of my life seemed to slip away with him.

A Gift for Perrier

Are you the sort of person who celebrates your dog's birthday with gifts? Do you go to your local pet supply store and browse through the shelves of squeaky toys, bones, biscuits and rawhides? Do you cook a steak for your dog's birthday or provide him with a favorite tidbit? I would have liked to have done all these things for Perrier's tenth birthday. However, Perrier was one of those dogs who did not play with toys and was on a restricted diet of cottage cheese and rice. I didn't dare break this diet, even for his special day. However, I did not anticipate the arrival of a special gift for his birthday.

Kimmel, a Labor Day "throw-away" kitten, appeared on our doorstep in time to make the perfect birthday gift for Ed's guide dog Perrier.

On the evening of September 4, 1989, Toni and I finished having dinner with our friend, Bobbie Mayer and her two daughters, Kimberly and Melia. When Kimberly went out to play, she found a kitten sitting on our doorstep. The kitten seemed hungry, but not starving, dirty or bedraggled. Kim and Melia begged us to keep the kitten. With great compassion Kim pleaded the kitten's case, stating he was unwanted, unloved and in need of a good home. Her comment was particularly poignant, since Kim, age eight, and Melia, age ten, were in the process of being adopted by Bobbie.

Friends checked lost and found ads and posted lost kitten signs for us in the neighborhood. No one claimed this black and white foundling. We named him Kimmel after Kimberly and Melia and decided he would be the perfect birthday present for Perrier, a living memorial to him and an extension of his spirit.

A congenial family portrait of Ed and Perrier, Toni and Ivy with family cats.   Avigdar Adams

Kimmel was not a replacement for Perrier; nor was Perrier's successor Kirby. Parting with my first guide dog was traumatic, but it helped me realize love is an unending process. My relationship with each new animal in my life is unique and I have discovered an unlimited capacity to love each as an individual. My grief over Perrier's death was not erased by my love for and ability to bond with Kimmel and Kirby. However, my joy in these new relationships did much to diminish my grief and refocus my love, energy and attention to new beginnings.

When Blindness Strikes

In June 1994 Ivy was seen by Dr. Alan MacMillan, a leading San Diego ophthalmologist, who comes to Fresno once a year to run eye clinics. Dr. Mac told us twelve-year-old Ivy had completely lost vision in her right eye but still had good vision in her left. Toni had noticed some hesitation and slowing down in Ivy's guiding but attributed it to Ivy's arthritis. This Delta Society Guide Dog of the Year award winner had continued to expertly perform her duties with such brilliance that Toni was unaware she was functioning with just one eye.

Several months later on a trip to Washington, D.C., to attend a conference, Ivy was her usual outstanding self for the first few days. On the last day of the meetings, Toni noticed a marked deterioration in Ivy's ability to guide. She was fine in the narrow corridors of the hotel, but when entering the open lobby area, she appeared confused and disoriented. At dusk she seemed particularly unsure of herself. Not wanting to put pressure on Ivy or endanger herself, Toni relied on sighted human guides and heeled Ivy for the rest of the trip.

Our trip back home was bittersweet. Toni knew the prognosis was not good and plans would have to be made to train with Ivy's successor. Ivy had been Toni's loyal guide for eleven years and had accumulated thousands of flying miles. Toni was teary throughout the flight home, knowing Ivy's retirement would soon be official.

In September we were scheduled to fly to San Diego to speak at the Tri-State (California, Nevada and Arizona) Veterinary Medical Association meetings and to receive a posthumous award for Kirby. This courageous Golden Retriever's amazing achievements are detailed in Chapter Eight and earned him a place in the California VMA's Animal Hall of Fame.

While in San Diego, we took Ivy to see Dr. Mac (as we called him). We had fantasized about corrective cataract surgery or other miraculous medical interventions, but Dr. Mac had to break the bad news that Ivy would soon be totally blind. In addition to cataracts and uveitis, she had inoperable retinal deterioration. As he described the condition, Ed experienced deja vu. While consulting an ophthalmologist twenty years earlier, Ed had heard a similar description of his failing eyesight!

The harsh and painful reality of Ivy's forced retirement was eased by our reunion with Robert Martinus, a British teenage friend who would be spending the next few months with us. Robert joined us in San Diego for some sightseeing but would make Fresno his home base. He took on the role of Toni's makeshift walking, talking, driving guide.

Several weeks after returning home, Ivy lost her remaining vision and became totally blind. She adjusted admirably to her disability. We were the ones struggling with deep emotions as a result of her condition. Although Ivy will remain with us in her retirement, the pain of shifting the bond from working partner to beloved pet is wrenching.

Goodbye

In March 1995 as Toni and I walked through Chicago's O'Hare Airport, my thoughts were swirling. Several weeks before this trip, I had made the decision to retire Kirby's successor Jake from guide service. As he competently guided me through the congested noisy airport, I began to have second thoughts about this decision. However, by the time we returned to Chicago two days later on our way home, my doubts were gone.

From the time I began my partnership with Jake in July 1994, he was somewhat distracted in the presence of dogs and cats while guiding me. He pulled so hard in harness, I frequently felt off-balance and uncomfortable. Unlike most Golden Retrievers, he did not enjoy being groomed, and daily obedience training sessions were a chore. Unlike most guide dogs, he resisted having his harness put on.

Despite these problems, Jake knew his basic guide work. His street crossings and traffic work were excellent. He was extremely bright and quickly learned new routes. In addition, he was a real gentleman in the house. Jake had been trained to relieve himself on leash and never forgot his early housetraining. He did not chew our possessions, did not steal food from tables or counters and was quiet and settled at home.

Not willing to give up easily, I sought help from several sources. Brad Scott, Director of Training at Leader Dogs, was in phone contact with me from the start. Brad, who had trained me with Jake, flew out to California in December in an effort to salvage us as a team.

An extremely flexible and experienced guide dog trainer, Brad was willing to incorporate many of the suggestions made to me by leading animal behaviorists. At first Brad and I tried breaking the distraction and pulling problems through the use of the Halti, a device similar to the halter used to control a headstrong horse. Unfortunately, Jake's reaction to the Halti was so negative that his guide work began to deteriorate. One of several techniques we employed was to drop the harness handle and put Jake at a sit when he began pulling. Another method was to drop the harness handle and heel Jake for several yards before picking up the handle and resuming formal guide work. A third suggestion, patterned after the way puppies are trained to heel, was to give Jake an about turn and reverse our direction. After walking several yards, we would do another about turn and resume our original direction. The premise for all these recommendations was the need to break Jake's concentration on whatever was distracting him and refocus his attention on me.

For eight months I experimented with these techniques, but it became increasingly apparent Jake was breaking down and I was losing confidence in him. At home he ignored our cats, Cameo, Kimmel and Kismet, but outside our home, cats became a fixation. Guide dogs are supposed to stop for curbs and steps, but not for cats streaking across their path. Noises began to stress Jake and he responded by pulling even more strongly when he heard a screeching siren, a slamming car door or barking dogs. If his work had been consistently bad, my decision to retire him would have been easier and made earlier. However, he did have good days and each such day gave me hope we were on the verge of a breakthrough.

In late January Toni and I went on a nine-day trip to Michigan, Florida and Texas. Like most of our trips, this one combined visits with friends and relatives with professional speaking engagements. In Lansing we spoke at the Michigan Veterinary Conference. Brad took this opportunity to join us for additional work with Jake and Ivy's successor Escort. Although pleased with the progress Escort was making since becoming Toni's guide six weeks earlier, Brad was distressed with the lack of progress Jake and I had made. For the first time in our many discussions about Jake, the subject of retiring him from guide work was introduced. I felt guilty that my poor dog-handling skills had exacerbated Jake's problems. Brad reassured me the difficulties were not created by me and my attempts to solve them showed a tremendous commitment to the relationship.

I still wasn't ready to consider breaking the bond until we flew from Michigan to Florida. Jake became uncontrollably anxious when our small commuter plane landed in Sarasota. When the door opened he became so frantic to get out, he neglected his role as guide. This incident confirmed my growing belief that Jake was no longer a safe and reliable guide. Once I faced the possibility of his retirement, I could talk about it openly. At our lecture to the veterinary students at Texas A&M, I reflected upon the probability of Jake's early retirement for work-related, rather than health, reasons. I received a great deal of support and understanding from the more than 100 students in attendance.

Brad did not seem surprised with my decision to retire Jake and said he would start looking for another dog. Realizing it would take some time before a new match could be made, I decided to continue working with Jake on a limited basis.

A month later Brad called with the news that Golden Retriever Echo, my soon-to-be partner, would arrive in Fresno on March 18th. Brad had plans to attend a meeting in Los Angeles, providing the opportunity for him to train me in my home setting. Jake was scheduled to go to his new home on March 17th.

Although our retirement plans were already set, Jake's excellent job of guiding through the airport rekindled my feelings of ambivalence. Even at this late date, I fantasized about a magic solution to our problem.

Our return trip to Fresno on the 16th was a mixture of sorrow and relief. By the end of this trip, I acknowledged my fantasies of

Jake enjoys his retirement as he and his Lhasa Apso pal, PJ, stare at a treed squirrel.
Sheila Cary

Jake's resuming his role as guide were just that, fantasies. Because our working relationship was rocky from the start, I never fell in love with him, but still grieved at the thought of breaking the bond.

Our friend Sheila Cary joined us for breakfast on the morning of the 17th. Learning of our need to retire Jake, Sheila had offered to adopt him. She planned to take Jake with her to work on a regular basis. Her house has a large yard in which Jake could romp with PJ, a Lhasa Apso. We knew Jake would be in good hands, but all three of us cried as Sheila prepared to leave with her new charge.

With the arrival of Echo the next day, my emotions shifted from sadness to anticipation. Jake has made a wonderful adjustment to his new lifestyle, and Echo gave early promise of developing into an outstanding guide.

Loss

How do you say goodbye to a legend? For me, Toni Eames, it was not without great pain and a deep sense of loss. On August 26, 1995, Ivy and I ended our twelve-year partnership.

In 1983, I received the devastating news that Flicka was terminally ill with lymphosarcoma and had only a few months to live. Totally committed to the breed, I wanted Flicka's successor to be another Golden Retriever. Not wanting to leave Flicka for the one month residential training at a school, I contracted with the former guide dog instructor who had trained Charm. Members of the Long Island Golden Retriever Club responded to my need by offering several potential candidates. Eleven-month-old Ivy won my heart because of her friendly disposition and responsiveness to training. Charm was mild and mellow, and Flicka frenetic. With her outgoing but controllable demeanor, Ivy's personality was appealing because it fell between these two extremes.

At the time Ivy became part of my family, I was living in Queens, New York, and commuting by railroad to my job at Kings Park Psychiatric Center. Ivy's apprenticeship began when she accompanied Flicka and me to work. With Flicka guiding on the left and Ivy heeling on the right, we must have been a striking threesome, although no one challenged my right to be accompanied by two guide dogs! In the following six months, Ivy was exposed to rail, subway and bus travel and the noise and confusion of congested city

The Eames' cats, Kismet, Kimmel and Cameo are fed on the kitchen counter to protect their food from the gluttony of their Golden Retriever housemates.   Sister Pauline Quinn

streets, and learned to lie quietly in theaters and restaurants. Ivy's public manners were exemplary, and by the time she took over from Flicka she was already familiar with the regular routes we traveled.

Ivy's new life was not all work. Like most Goldens, she was passionate about tennis balls. Dorothy Dengel took Ivy out for a run and game of fetch during break time. Patients often joined Dorothy and Ivy in these games and received great pleasure from Ivy's responsiveness to them. Back in my office Ivy provided pet therapy to the more withdrawn patients.

Ivy was a confirmed cat lover. When she joined my family I shared my home with two tabbies, Disney and Tevye. Although Tevye and Ivy never developed much of a relationship, she and Disney became playmates. One of Ivy's favorite games was to poke her nose under Disney's sleeping body and flip him over. After moving to California, Ivy welcomed Cameo into the family. This eight-year-old, black and white cat had been an only pet until my mother's death. Recognizing Cameo's reluctance to interact with other animals, Ivy was respectful of Cameo's need for space.

Everyone needs a best friend with whom to share secrets. After first meeting Ed, I shared with Ivy my fantasy of marrying this warm and humorous professor. Over the next few months, Ivy guided me on the two hour commute from my office to Ed's to collaborate on our guide dog book. The dream I shared with Ivy came true when she and Perrier were attendants at our wedding.

Two years after our move to California, Ivy lost Perrier, her playmate and traveling buddy. Ivy, an alpha dog, was somewhat possessive about her toys. Fortunately, Ed's new guide Kirby was a Zeta and treated Ivy as an adored older sister. He followed her around, longingly eyeing every toy she held in her mouth. As soon as she dropped that toy, he would zero in on it until she picked up a new one.

Ivy and Kirby not only competed for toys, but also competed in the Obedience ring. Shortly after our dogs' Obedience triumphs, our family was thrown into the depths of despair as a consequence of devastating disease. Within several weeks of each other, my adored cat Disney and Ed's partner Kirby were diagnosed with cancer. After Disney's surgery he developed a serious virus which was transmitted to Cameo. Our household was in complete turmoil, especially after the amputation of Kirby's front leg. During this crisis, Ivy remained one of the stabilizing forces in our lives.

Ivy was the consummate professional. Her exemplary demeanor at numerous legislative hearings in California helped foster laws expanding the rights of people with disabilities teamed with privately trained assistance dogs.

When blindness struck, the brilliant and adaptable Ivy assumed the honored and well-earned title of Guide Dog Emeritus. For the next year she resumed her position on my right side as her successor, Escort, took over the guide position on my left. The indomitable Ivy learned to navigate as a blind dog and continued to accompany us to many familiar places around town.

When we traveled outside of Fresno, several friends volunteered for Ivy-sitting duties. During our July 1995 trip to South Dakota and New York, she stayed with Helen and Beth Shea. I told everyone Ivy was at summer camp because she got to swim almost every day in Helen's pool. It comforts me to know that two weeks before her death, Ivy had a last fling by indulging in one of her favorite passions.

After our return from this trip, Ivy was diagnosed with cardiomyopathy and began retaining fluid. On August 26th, for the first time in her life, Ivy, a glutton for food, refused to eat. I needed no clearer sign it was time for me to let her go. I phoned our veterinarian, Bob Larsen, and asked him to come to our home for the euthanasia. As I hung up the phone and began sobbing, fourteen-year-old Cameo sprang into action. She flung herself into my arms with a clear message that she felt my pain and was there to comfort me. When my tears dried, I sat on the floor stroking Ivy, and Cameo shared her ministrations with her long-term house partner. She walked back and forth between Ivy and me purring loudly and stopping periodically to lick Ivy's face, something she had never done before.

When Dr. Larsen and our friend Eve Hoopes arrived, we all sat in a circle around Ivy to comfort her in her last moments. Cameo, who had been fast asleep, jumped over Eve to play her part. She laid facing Ivy and soothingly purred her into death.

How do I say goodbye to a legend? My way of honoring Ivy's memory is to shower her successors with love and devotion and help them live up to her outstanding example.

Chapter Ten

Reestablishing the Partnership

R elinquishing the partnership with a working canine as a result of death, disease or early retirement is traumatic. For some, the shock may be so stressful that they refuse to seek partnership with a successor dog. However, the vast majority of us feel the benefits of working with canine assistants far outweigh the negatives, including the grief when the partnership ends.

In the following sections, we draw upon our own experience to illuminate the process of moving on to establish new relationships. Ed's loss of Perrier led to a partnership with Kirby, who eventually made guide dog history by becoming the first three-legged working guide. For Toni, the transition to working with Escort was made easier by Ivy's forced retirement due to blindness and the time Toni waited for her new partner. In contrast, the failure of Ed and Jake to become an effective team had an impact on his relationship with Echo.

Changing Partners

Imagine sitting across the breakfast table from your partner of eight years basking in the comfort of familiarity. Your bacon, eggs, toast and coffee are done to perfection because you know each other's tastes so well. The scene shifts, imagine that your partner is gone and a stranger is facing you. You like his looks, but you don't know much about him. This scenario is played out when disabled people face the death or retirement of their familiar canine partners. This transition took place for me, Ed, after Perrier's death.

At my first meeting with Perrier I was overwhelmed by his size. Every time he opened his huge mouth to yawn, I drew back in horror! Actually, he was a very gentle black Labrador, and we had eight years of wonderful togetherness.

Three weeks after Perrier's death, I traveled to Palm Springs, California to train at Guide Dogs of the Desert (GDD). There, on November 22, 1989, I met Kirby. I had not heard of the Kirby vacuum cleaner, but when Kirby became my partner, I was immediately bombarded with a variety of vacuum cleaner jokes.

Kirby was an eighty-pound teddy bear of a Golden. As he sniffed me, I ran my hands over his furry body. His tail intrigued me as it curled over his back. Despite this cosmetic fault, it was love at first touch!

An aspect of training at GDD I particularly liked was the emphasis placed on obedience. While students practiced daily obedience, instructors tossed tennis balls to one another, played with cats and puppies, and even held choice morsels of food directly in front of the dogs. Since cats were already part of my household, I was given a cat to hold while going through obedience exercises with Kirby. In this and many other parts of the training, instructors stressed dealing with distracting conditions rather than avoiding them.

Although I loved Kirby's temperament and personality from the moment of our first meeting, bonding, based on trust as well as love, took longer. One week before graduation, Kirby and I were crossing a busy intersection. Kirby suddenly stopped and I heard screeching brakes as a car stopped inches from our bodies. This three-year-old Golden was the only calm participant in the drama. After we crossed the intersection, my instructor explained that the driver made a left turn into the intersection and the sun blinded her for a few seconds. If Kirby had not stopped, both of us would have been seriously injured. From that time on, Kirby was my own personal WONDER DOG.

Kirby never learned how I like my bacon, eggs and coffee, but he became part of our family and I looked forward to many years of a loving partnership.

My New Escort

The anticipation of working with a new partner is both joyous and stressful. As arthritis took its toll on Ivy, she rarely engaged in games of fetch or showed enthusiasm when I, Toni, reached for her harness. The thought of a young, eager and playful dog was exciting. On the other hand, after eleven years of working together, Ivy and I were a skilled and experienced team. The idea of starting over with an inexperienced and unseasoned canine assistant was daunting.

After blindness forced her retirement, Ivy passed the torch of her outstanding career as a guide dog to her successor, Escort. Brad Scott

Because Ed's experience at Leader Dogs had been so positive, I turned to that organization for Ivy's successor. Knowing my breed-specific preferences, Brad Scott, Director of Training, scoured the kennels for a suitable Golden Retriever. Having located my dream dog, Brad called to provide details of the forthcoming match. My future partner was a seventy-five-pound two-year-old male who had been donated to Leader as an adult dog. Brad's enthusiasm about this dog was infectious.

I noticed, however, he was reticent about using the dog's name. When at my urging Brad revealed my dream dog's name, the reason for his reluctance became apparent. This would be the second dog named Jake to become a member of our household within a year. Brad had expected me to be disappointed to learn there was a Jake Two headed my way. Much to his surprise, I responded with delight and changed his name on the spot. This was my chance to indulge a long-held fancy to have a guide called Escort. I imagined how classy it would be to respond to an invitation by saying "I'll be there with my Escort" or "My Escort and I would be happy to accept your invitation." Little did I realize the younger generation would assume he was named after an automobile!

My low thyroid condition makes adjustments to extremes of temperature unmanageable. Therefore, training with a new dog during a Michigan winter would be impossible. My problem was solved when Brad came to Fresno to work with Ed, who was having serious adjustment problems with Jake. Since Brad was already scheduled to come to California, he was able to bring Escort with him and train me at home. Under special circumstances, Leader does fifteen to twenty "home deliveries" a year. Ed and I are strong advocates of home training since the team becomes familiar with the environment in which they will live and work.

On December 15, 1994, our training began. When it was time to go out, this bundle of energetic silliness thrust his head into the harness and turned into a focused professional working dog. His pace was slow and steady and he was totally concentrated on his job as guide. Accompanied by Brad and sometimes by Ed and Jake, we took walks in the neighborhood, expanding our routes to include our local shopping mall, the airport and some of our favorite restaurants. We took the bus to the bank and to City Hall where we attend monthly meetings of disability-related advisory councils. Day by day our confidence in each other mounted and we began to grow together as a team. Although inexperienced, Escort was a quick and willing learner and met all my expectations for Ivy's successor.

Before Brad returned to Michigan, we made a day trip to San Francisco. During this sixteen-hour excursion, Escort and Jake encountered a wide variety of normal urban conditions. We traveled by train (Amtrak) and subway (BART) to San Francisco. In the city we walked through the crowds along Fisherman's Wharf, maneuvering around street vendors and sidewalk stands. Escort took every new experience in stride and only exhibited excitement when we approached the waterfront on Pier 39. Demonstrating his Golden Retriever heritage, Escort let me know he would love to join the sea gulls for a swim.

Saying goodbye to Brad left me with mixed emotions. Working with him was fun and his presence provided a sense of security in my fledgling partnership with Escort. With Brad's departure, my Escort and I were on our own to handle travel problems as they arose.

Rebounding With Echo

Our household is beginning to get noisy and boisterous again. When Jake was retired, Escort lost a wrestling partner and playmate. The day after Jake left our home to start his new life as a pet, Echo arrived in Fresno to start his new life as Ed's guide. Brad was scheduled to attend a meeting in Los Angeles in late March and flew to California a week early to work with Echo and me.

Poor Brad did not escape from a cold, wintry Michigan to a warm sunny California. Almost every day we set out to practice in different areas within walking distance of my home and invariably got caught in a downpour. Echo must have thought he was in Seattle! Despite Toni's admonitions to wear our rain gear, Brad and I blithely left the house each day under the delusion that yesterday's drenching signaled the end of the rainy season. Despite the horrible weather, Brad, Echo and I mastered the familiar routes traversed by Toni and Escort three months earlier.

Unlike Escort who barreled into Toni's life, twenty-two-month-old Echo was more subtle in his affection. In true Golden Retriever fashion, he loves to cuddle and lie on my feet. When at home and off duty, Escort sporadically displays a high level of energetic silliness which, thankfully, Echo does not emulate. Like Escort, Echo came to Fresno with a thick, luxurious coat, a result of the Michigan winter. With summer temperatures in the three-digit range, Echo will probably follow Escort's lead and lose his thick undercoat which makes the top coat so gorgeous!

After six weeks of routine walks in familiar areas, we took off on our first cross-country adventure. Echo had previously experienced air travel when he flew to Fresno with Brad. However, this was our maiden voyage as a working team. The American Airlines ground and air crews gave Echo a welcome befitting visiting royalty. Initially my new canine partner was somewhat uneasy but settled down and took jet travel in his stride.

Our first port of call was Columbus, Ohio where Toni and I were to be honored by *Newsreel*. After Kirby's death, we established a memorial fund to raise money for this interactive cassette magazine by and for blind people. One of the unanticipated pleasures of this trip was the fun we had walking around downtown Columbus. Escort and Echo experienced urban life as they guided us through people rushing about their business, heavy traffic, screeching sirens and lots of street noise.

From Ohio we flew to Alabama, where we did a series of presentations for the staff and students at the Tuskegee University veterinary school. Although Echo quickly adapted to jet travel, he was less than thrilled with travel on small, commuter prop planes. He was restless and failed to maintain a Down Stay. However, by the time we boarded the fourth commuter plane in thirty-eight hours, he was more relaxed and settled in for the flight.

Our last stop took us to Michigan where we spent several days working with Brad at Leader. He was impressed with how well Echo and I were doing.

An aspect of training we focused on was traffic work. Brad drove a vehicle to test Echo's steadiness in traffic. As we walked along a specified route, Brad carried out a variety of checks. At one point he pulled out of a driveway across our path. While crossing a street he made a sudden turn in front of us. Another time he cut us off by pulling out of a parking lot. Guide dogs do not monitor traffic lights; they respond to moving objects such as cars, bicycles, baby carriages, shopping carts or pedestrians. Echo proved his competence in handling these traffic checks. After our training session, Larry, a training supervisor, repeated Brad's driving maneuvers with Toni and Escort. As usual, Escort was the total professional.

On our return home, the Golden boys resumed their suburban lifestyle without even missing a beat.

Chapter Eleven

Expanding the Partnership:
Obedience Training and Competition

Prior to Toni's training of her first guide dog for AKC Obedience competition, no blind person handling a guide dog in the ring had successfully competed for Obedience titles. Working with different

Ed and Kirby practicing the off-lead at heeling exercise. Kirby earned a CDX several months after Ivy.
Karen Newcomb

Practicing for AKC Open competition, Toni takes the dumbbell from Ivy. Ivy was the first guide dog handled by a blind partner to receive the CDX title.
Karen Newcomb

trainers at the Novice level, Toni was able to earn Companion Dog (CD) Obedience titles with Charm and Flicka. With Ivy, she went beyond this commendable feat and earned a Companion Dog Excellent (CDX) title at the Open, or intermediate, level.

We believe the bond between guide dog and blind partner is reinforced by any activity enhancing their work as a team. Obedience training and competition certainly is one way to do this. Since our entry into the competitive Obedience world, several other blind competitors have entered this arena of sporting activity.

Novice Obedience Competition

When I met my husband Ed in 1984, he was unfamiliar with the world of dogs. Although he had been working with Perrier for three years, he knew little about dog behavior and training. He had a surprising reaction to my boast that my previous guide dogs had earned CDs. Obviously puzzled, Ed said he did not realize banks issued certificates of deposit to dogs! Wow, this man needed educating!

Several years after getting Charm, I joined the Long Island Golden Retriever Club where I met Laurie Doumaux, an Obedience trainer. Working with Laurie, I began working toward the fulfillment of a long-held dream—competing with Charm in AKC Obedience Trials. Laurie adapted her training techniques to work effectively with a blind handler. As Charm and I perfected our Novice work under Laurie's tutelage, we were faced with a major barrier—changing the AKC Obedience regulations to accommodate disabled handlers.

AKC staffers were excited about the innovative concept of a blind handler competing in Obedience. Working closely with Laurie and me, they clarified the rules to accommodate a blind person's need for guidance in the ring and auditory posts in the figure eight exercise.

In 1972, Charm earned her Companion Dog title in three Trials. Two factors worked against my continuing into Open competition with her. She was seven years old and unaccustomed to jumping, an activity necessary for intermediate level Obedience competition. Secondly, Laurie, who had freely given her time and expertise to working with us, was moving to Virginia.

Escort is shown here preparing for AKC Obedience competition. In the area behind their town house, Toni and Escort work on the figure eight exercise with Ed and Obedience trainer Deb Harper serving as auditory posts.   Sister Pauline Quinn

After Charm's death, my friend Paul Gabias and I began training her successor. Once I felt confident Flicka had mastered the role of guide dog, I searched for a trainer who would work with us on competitive Obedience. Many highly qualified and competent trainers were available in the New York area where I worked and lived. However, I needed a trainer who was willing to meet my special needs. Foremost among these was the need to meet my commuter train after work, drive Flicka and me to a practice area, work with us privately and return us in time to catch a later train home. In 1981 when Flicka was five, I met Ann Strathern, a friend of Laurie's.

Ann and I faced a formidable challenge in training Flicka for competition. Once her harness and leash were removed, Flicka became a virtual whirling dervish. Released from her responsibilities as guide, she would leap into the air, race circles around us and fling herself into our arms. We never knew whether to laugh at her acrobatic exuberance or try to stop her. The thought of turning this dynamo into a controlled Obedience competitor was awesome. Every time she displayed her unbounded canine energy at the beginning of a training session, I marveled at the ease with which she could transfer that energy into the constraints of the guide dog role.

Before learning to stand for examination, heel off-leash or return on a recall, Flicka had to be convinced I had the same control of her off the leash as I did when she was on leash. In contrast to Charm, who needed to be motivated by a great deal of praise, Flicka needed to be controlled by a calm, unemotional approach. When she earned praise, my "Good girl" was delivered in a whisper! Despite our trepidation, Flicka, like her predecessor, received her CD title in just three Trials.

Ann was a glutton for punishment and agreed to continue with us helping prepare for Open competition. Certain exercises presented no problems. As a guide dog, Flicka was frequently required to sit or down for long periods of time. My being out of sight did not disturb her. Flicka wore a bell during training so I could hear her movements during the drop on recall exercise. For me, the most difficult exercise was the retrieve over the high jump. I found it difficult to throw the dumbbell consistently straight over the jump. Without a sighted person around to retrieve my crooked throws and to help correct my aim, I was unable to practice this activity as frequently as I would have liked. Once Ann thought I was ready to compete, we could concentrate our efforts on Flicka.

My creative dynamo invented many variations in the performance of the jumping exercise. She jumped one way, but not the other; she jumped both ways without picking up the dumbbell; she jumped one way, retrieved the dumbbell and brought it to Ann; and, most frustrating of all, she jumped both ways, retrieved the dumbbell, and out of sheer joy of having "mastered" the exercise, raced circles around me. Because of my blindness, I could not respond immediately to these infractions, which made my corrections less effective.

Training Flicka continued to be a challenge to Ann's and my ingenuity. Just weeks away from entering our first Open Trial, I received a terrible blow. Flicka was diagnosed with terminal cancer and the chemotherapeutic drugs she was taking made her too weak to compete.

A year after my partnership with Ivy began, I met Ed and Perrier. As I shared my dreams of CDs and CDXs with him, I could feel his enthusiasm for Obedience competition growing. Unfortunately for us, Ann had moved to Maryland shortly after Flicka's death.

We put thoughts of competitive training on the back burner while we settled into our new life in Fresno. As our thoughts turned back to training, we had to face the tragedy of Perrier's illness and subsequent euthanasia. Several months passed, during which Ed trained with Kirby and devoted the time necessary for them to become an effective working team.

In 1990 we met Jo Amenda, our "successor" trainer, who was delighted and enthusiastic about working with us. Ed and I began working with Jo in the spring and were ready for competition in September. We worked with Jo twice a week, once privately and once as part of a class. Classes met weekly at a park near our home, but our private sessions were held at a variety of parks in Fresno. For me, working with a class was a totally new experience. However, the advantages were soon obvious. Students could observe and help each other and the dogs could be proofed under all kinds of distracting conditions.

One problem has plagued me throughout my career as an Obedience competitor; I find it impossible to walk a straight line. This tendency did not adversely affect my dogs as long as we worked in open spaces. However, in a ring, where veering could result in walking into a ring rope, scissor gate or wall, my dogs' guide training took over. Ivy, like her predecessors, was a good heeler until she thought my safety was jeopardized. She got nervous and as a result, her heeling deteriorated. For Ed, who lost his sight later in life, walking a straight line in open areas is not a problem. However, in an indoor ring where sounds rebound, he is as disoriented as I.

Whether in practice or at a show, we have to make the judge aware of our needs. The judge must make sure we do not collide with ring barriers. In the figure eight exercise, the ring stewards provide an auditory signal by repeating "Post, post, post." so we can walk around them. A steward can guide us back to our dogs on the stand for examination and can guide us in the ring to position us for the start of a new exercise. Either a steward or a fellow competitor can guide us across the ring and back to our dogs on the long sits and long downs.

On September 1, 1990 we entered our first show. When the judge called my number for a run-off, I was incredulous. Although I lost the run-off to a classmate, I was delighted to place fourth with a score of 195½. I was extremely proud of Ed, who, in his very first show, scored 193½. A score of 200 indicates a perfect performance.

The next day we were fortunate to have an equally relaxed and enthusiastic judge. From the beginning of my work with Jo, I teased her about outscoring her someday. When Ivy and I scored 195½ again, we took second place, while Jo and her Golden Retriever took third. Ed and Kirby took fourth with an improved score of 194.

We did not compete for our third leg until November because we traveled to the United Kingdom in September to study the guide dog movement there, and to the Delta Society meeting in Houston in October. On November 17th, when Ed and I competed for our third and final leg, we encountered unanticipated conditions. We had only practiced outdoors, and Ivy and Kirby had never worked on mats. My inability to walk a straight line caused me to step on and off the mats during this indoor Trial. Ivy's concern over what she perceived to be unsafe footing made her nervous and her heeling was erratic. In contrast to our two previous shows, the judge at this one was nervous and uncertain about working with blind handlers. Ivy and I scored 189½, while Kirby and Ed scored 191.

For the first time in AKC history, two guide dogs handled by their blind partners simultaneously earned CDs.

Open Obedience Competition

When Ivy and Kirby earned their CDs, we jumped into Open work with gusto. In contrast with Novice training where we could practice independently, some of the Open exercises required sighted assistance and specially adapted devices. Behind our town house is a small lawn area where we did the bulk of our training. Once a week, we practiced in a park or school yard with a class under the direction of the aforementioned Jo Amenda.

In order to prevent confusion between the roles of working guide and Obedience competitor, the dogs wear different collars and leads for each activity. Although Open heeling is done off lead, when we practiced by ourselves, we used short leads to insure the dogs remained in position. Initially, when training for the drop on recall, the dogs wore bells on their collars so we could determine whether they dropped. This method proved inadequate when we needed to reward and release them from the down position. Unless they were panting hard, the bells stopped ringing once they dropped. We turned to a friend for assistance.

Howard Hurtt listened to our problem and came up with a clever solution. He created small beeping boxes attached to Velcro straps that could be placed around the dogs' necks. Not only could we tell the instant the dogs dropped, but we could locate them and give food rewards. The beeping boxes were also useful while practicing the long sits and downs. Bells on their collars alerted us to the dogs moving out of position, while the beeping boxes enabled us to return to the dogs at the end of the exercise. When not in use, a plug stopped the beeping sound and the devices could be recharged whenever necessary.

Obedience trainer Deb Harper does the preliminary work in teaching Echo the basics of the high jump.   Sister Pauline Quinn

Howard also designed a beeping dumbbell which Ed used when training Kirby to retrieve. Ivy was already a reliable retriever and took great joy in working with her dumbbell. Although Kirby, a true Golden Retriever, enjoyed carrying toys in his mouth, he had no formal fetch training. He was happy to take the dumbbell from hand, but when thrown, would not chase and retrieve it. By substituting the beeping dumbbell, Ed knew where it was and could more readily enforce his fetch command. Before getting this device, Ed had no way of knowing Kirby had disobeyed the fetch command until he returned empty-mouthed. Using the beeping device, Ed could immediately determine Kirby had retrieved and was returning with the dumbbell.

An unanticipated advantage of Howard's creation was that it improved Toni's ability to throw the dumbbell. Although several classmates tried to teach her to throw underhand, it just didn't work. By throwing it overhand, she had greater consistency in throwing straight. Leaving the dogs in the house and using the beeping mechanism, Toni could practice throwing and retrieving her own dumbbell!

Despite purchasing a set of jumps to practice on our own, we discovered the impossibility of practicing these exercises without sighted assistance. At first, Toni stood next to the high jump hoping to hear the thud of Kirby's landing when he took the jump. Although this method sometimes worked, it was not dependable. When Ed listened for Ivy's thud, the method was even less reliable due to her lighter weight. The broad jump presented an even greater problem. We abandoned attempting to practice these exercises on our own because we didn't want to praise the dogs if they didn't take the jumps.

Deb Harper, a trainer working with Jo, came to our rescue. Two or three times a week, Deb came to our house and provided the sighted assistance we needed to practice the Open exercises. In her role as training coach, she helped us prepare the dogs for competition.

In the Open ring we needed additional accommodations beyond those needed in the Novice class. Because we have difficulty walking a straight line indoors, we requested removal of the jumps during the heeling pattern. In our training we have been encouraged to move swiftly in the ring to keep the dogs' attention focused on us. However, experience taught us some judges failed to stop us before

Toni and Ivy earn the CDX title with a first place win at the Kings KC of California. At the same show, Ed and Kirby earn their first CDX leg with a fourth place win. Mitchell

we collided with the ring ropes. The jumps in the ring during the heeling pattern would be an additional threat to our safety. During the drop on recall exercise, when many judges use hand signals, we needed voice signals. Since correct positioning of dog and handler during the high and broad jump exercises is essential, we needed someone familiar with the positions we assumed during practice to position us.

We wrote to the AKC and they found our requests for accommodation reasonable. They reasoned these modifications did not give us or the dogs an unfair advantage in the ring. Most judges were comfortable working with us, but some were noticeably nervous judging blind handlers.

Deb was the pivotal element in our Open efforts. In addition to the individualized training sessions, she chauffeured us to out-of-town shows. Besides showing her Golden Retriever, Sage, for Obedience Trial Champion (OTCH) points and trying to put an advanced Obedience title (Utility Dog) on a friend's Golden, Deb assisted us in the ring. Her most important role was correctly placing us for the high and broad jumps. When judges preferred giving hand signals for the drop on recall, Deb provided verbal signals.

Whether working in the ring or guiding in harness, Ivy and Kirby's performance styles were very different. Ivy was very serious and showed concern when she made a mistake. Kirby, on the other hand, was happy-go-lucky and largely unconcerned when his performance in the ring was not up to par. Therefore, Ivy was easier to train and earned her CDX title in eight shows. Kirby had fun in the ring and invariably drew a comment from the judge about how energetic and animated he was in the ring. Whether he declined to participate in heeling, ignored Ed's request to drop on recall, regarded the high jump as a one-way trip, pretended never to have been taught the broad jump or feigned exhaustion on the sit stay, he never stopped smiling and wagging his tail. Of course, Ed contributed to some of these ring fiascoes. Poor Kirby was terribly confused when Ed told him to Jump instead of Fetch in the retrieve on the flat exercise. On another occasion, Ed was sure Kirby had not qualified (NQ) when he had to give a second Heel command and, therefore, sing-songed his Come command on the next exercise. When Ed repeated the command (a definite NQ) in his normal voice, Kirby did a flawless recall, an immediate drop, a straight front (a rare occurrence) and a perfect return to heel. The result of all this goofing off was Ed and Kirby raised the national average for the number of Trials needed to earn the title!

Although Ivy's Open scores (187, 191 and 193) were not as high as in Novice, she earned a first and third placement in the course of earning her title. Kirby got his first leg and a fourth place (187) at the same show in which Ivy finished her CDX and took first place. Ed was getting discouraged and losing hope, but when Kirby got a second leg with a 187½, Ed's spirits revived. Many entry fees, restaurant meals, hotel rooms and miles later, Ed was overjoyed when Kirby earned his third leg, despite the less-than-outstanding score of 180!

Competing in Bermuda

When we decided to compete with the dogs in Bermuda, we wondered how we could manage in the ring without Deb. She offered to stow away in our luggage, but we found a more practical solution. By measuring the exact distance between the dogs and the jumps, we could let the judges in Bermuda know precisely where to position us and the dogs for the jumping exercises. Happily, this technique proved successful for all concerned.

Our trip to Bermuda was sponsored by the World Congress of Kennel Clubs, where we were invited speakers. This invitation also provided the opportunity to participate in Bermuda's fabled dog shows. Elfreda Lines, the Bermuda Dog Training Club member coordinating our visit, filled us in on the requirements for competing in Obedience Trials. We would need copies of Ivy's and Kirby's AKC registration certificates and official three-generation pedigrees in order to register them with the Bermuda Kennel Club.

Even though our dogs had participated in AKC Open competition, they would have to earn their Bermuda CDs before going on to compete in Open there. As soon as dogs earn three legs and qualify for a title, they can immediately bump up to the next level of competition. By scheduling five days of shows, the Bermuda Kennel Club cleverly hooks the dog show fanatic into returning to the island to complete the second title. In response to these requirements, we began practicing both Novice and Open exercises.

On the first day of Trials, Charles Vaucrosson, a member of the Lions Club, picked us up at our hotel and drove us to the Botanical Gardens where the show was being held. We arrived early and took the opportunity to speak with the three judges about the accommodations we would need in the ring. AKC judges Jack Ward and Jack Volhard and Canadian Kennel Club judge Freda Walls were delighted to have us in their rings.

Kay Collins, Obedience show chairperson, took us under her wing. For the next five days, she helped us warm up the dogs after "pooping them" (her term), escorted us to the bathroom and to the coffee truck. Kay narrated Ed and Kirby's ring performance for Toni and did the same for Ed when Toni and Ivy were in the ring. We enjoyed these ebullient narrations tinged with Kay's musical Scottish accent.

Our resumption of Novice training in Fresno paid off and both dogs qualified for their CDs in three Trials. In fact, Kirby earned a third place on the first day of competition. On the fourth day, the dogs competed in Open. Ivy qualified and earned a third place, but Kirby failed to take the broad jump. On day five, they reversed with Kirby qualifying and Ivy cutting the corner on the broad jump. We found the atmosphere, both outside and within the ring, much more relaxed than at AKC Trials.

The final day of dog shows was sponsored by the World Congress. That evening, we attended an awards banquet where, to our delight, Kirby received a trophy for highest scoring Golden in Trial. The trophy was presented to Ed and Kirby by Prince Michael of Kent, patron of the World Congress. Prince Michael is first cousin to Queen Elizabeth. We got to chat with the Prince the next night at a cocktail party for Congress participants held at the governor's mansion. The Prince petted Ivy and Kirby, the only dogs present, as he told us about his two pet Labradors.

The next evening, a party was given by the Premier. Our intention was to stay for only a short while. However, Prince Michael made an unscheduled appearance and we learned etiquette requires that no one leaves a party before royalty. Royalist Bermudians informed us this etiquette was not to be breached even if one had a plane to catch.

At these cocktail parties we met Neal Berney, Bermuda Department of Agriculture chief veterinarian, and questioned him about the Bermudian stand on the lack of a quarantine. In order to maintain their rabies-free environments, Hawaii, the United Kingdom and many other islands have imposed lengthy quarantines. Neal explained since Bermuda has no indigenous wildlife population, such as raccoons, squirrels and rabbits, the threat of the spread of rabies is minimal. Furthermore, the income from tourists attending Bermuda's biannual dog shows is substantial. Understandably, the imposition of a quarantine would hurt the shows and the financial benefits generated by them.

The cocktail parties also provided the opportunity to meet delegates from the kennel clubs of Australia, the United Kingdom, Canada and Finland. We met and got to socialize with fellow World Congress speakers. During the course of the Congress, Ann Jeglum, a veterinarian from Pennsylvania, presented research material about the high incidence of cancer in Golden Retrievers. Roger Mugford, animal behaviorist from England, spoke about the impact of nutrition on behavior. Ian Dunbar, the well-known California-based veterinarian and animal behaviorist, discussed techniques to avert and to control aggression in dogs. Several evenings after the close of Congress activities, the Bermuda Dog Training Club hosted sessions in which Ian's training videos were shown and he answered questions from the audience.

A topic generating considerable controversy was the dangerous dog legislation in the U.K. Members of the American delegation voiced objections to the necessity for breed-specific legislation. They contended dogs should be judged by their behavior, not their genealogy.

We keep in touch with many of the friends we met during that memorable trip to Bermuda. Now that Escort and Echo have begun training for Obedience competition, we look forward to returning to this gorgeous island and its kind people as often as we can.

Chapter Twelve

Who Has Rights?

Recognizing the essential activities assistance dogs perform for their disabled partners, state and federal laws have been passed guaranteeing the right of access to all places of public accommodation for the team. That includes all forms of public transportation, hotels, eating establishments, medical facilities, schools and the work place. Unfortunately, the passage of laws does not guarantee compliance with them.

Because of their longer history and public exposure, guide dogs have fewer access problems than hearing and service dogs. However, this does not mean everyone recognizes the functions of a guide dog.

When faced with the problem of access denial, several alternatives are available to the disabled partner. One is to walk away from the confrontation and go elsewhere. This is a possibility for restaurants and hotels, but more problematic for work, school or hospitals. Another alternative is to try to educate the person denying access. Many disabled people remain committed to this route, but some get tired of needing to take the time and energy to continually play the role of educator. Some take legal action in enforcing their rights. Frequently, this is a long and tortuous process. Unfortunately, a few terminate their present partnerships or choose not to seek partnerships with successor dogs to avoid these unpleasant confrontations.

Despite the positive educational experiences of youngsters like Joe Reed and Kellie Christenson, (see Chapter Seven), some educational authorities have attempted to deny access to youngsters partnered with service dogs. An additional setting in which problems have emerged is medical facilities.

Hospital access denials fall into three categories: disabled people as employees, as visitors or as patients. As visitors, few problems are found in gaining access to most sections of hospitals. As employees, some complaints have been received about restrictive policies. In one Oregon hospital, although visitors with guide dogs were welcome to use the front door entrance, a blind employee with a guide dog was barred from using the same entrance. However, the vast majority of problems are faced by hospitalized patients wanting their assistance dogs with them. Despite the difficulties, some patients, like Mary Hook and Nemo (see Chapter Six), have progressive medical teams who understood their need to have their dogs close by.

If hospitals and schools are institutional settings in which access rights have sometimes been denied, zoos represent an intriguing arena where the rights of disabled people and the welfare of animals have been seen by some as conflicting.

Going to the Zoo

In November, 1993, a woman with a seizure disorder partnered with a service dog filed a complaint with the United States Department of Justice (DOJ) against the San Diego Zoo for denying her access with her dog. According to the complaintant, this was a clear violation of the Americans with Disabilities Act (ADA).

The DOJ lawyer investigating her complaint asked us to provide background information. On December 28, 1993, Ed wrote in part:

> In exploring the diversity of zoo policies regarding assistance dogs and the reasons suggested for these policies, I realized there were several myths created to justify denial of access. These are usually based upon the "what if" syndrome and are rarely rooted in reality. Like many myths developed to justify paternalistic policies, these are based upon the suggestion that the institution is only "protecting" disabled people.
>
> MYTH 1   Assistance dogs might become so excited or frightened by zoo animals they might cause injury to their disabled partners. Under such conditions, the zoo might be liable for the injury.
>
> MYTH 2   Assistance dogs might get so excited, they would break away from their disabled

partners and frighten or attack the zoo animals.

MYTH 3   Zoo animals would get so frightened by the presence of an assistance dog, they might, in terror, injure or kill themselves. Sometimes, this argument is reinforced by the experience of packs of wild dogs invading some zoos and creating havoc.

MYTH 4   Some animals, particularly those from Australia, might see dogs as natural enemies and might respond by flight or attack. It is argued that in Australia the dingo is a natural enemy and dogs are similar to dingoes.

MYTH 5   The presence of assistance dogs might result in the transmission of cross-species diseases. Thus, assistance dogs could transmit canine diseases to zoo animals and vice versa.

The first three reasons are based on invalid assumptions about the training and behavior of assistance dogs, the inability of disabled people to control their canine partners and the response of zoo animals. In fact, almost every expert I have consulted has suggested young children and many adults present more of a threat to zoo animals than any assistance dog or group of trained dogs could. Assistance dogs cannot be equated with wild dog packs which have on occasion invaded zoo grounds and caused considerable damage and injury to resident animals.

Most veterinarians, except those employed by zoos denying access, scoff at the cross-species disease potential introduced by assistance dogs. They suggest that because assistance dogs live indoors and receive regular veterinary care, they present less of a danger to zoo populations than does the general public.

The San Diego Zoo went on the public relations warpath and got favorable coverage of their discriminatory policy from local television stations and newspapers. A picture was painted of rare and endangered species self-destructing or failing to breed because of the presence of assistance dogs. However, zoo representatives did admit most other zoos in the country welcomed these highly-trained canine assistants and had faced no problems with their exhibit animals.

On March 10, 1994 the controversy hit the national press when the *Wall Street Journal* published an editorial supporting the San Diego Zoo. In its attack on the ADA, the editorial states:

> Everyone involved recognizes the importance of a guide or service dog to the disabled person, including the sense of independence that such assistance affords. But here, as in so many potential rubs with the disabilities law, the situation cries out for common sense, including a realization that nature will not allow all the disabled reasonably to join in every single activity that they might wish. Mr. Jouett (zoo spokesperson) says about five visitors a month bring assistance dogs to the zoo and affiliated wilderness park, against more than 350,000 who don't. At some point, able-bodied people's prerogatives count, too.

By portraying the complaint lodged by a woman with a seizure disorder as an example of the tyranny of the minority over the majority, the *Wall Street Journal* overlooked the facts of the case. In contrast to the San Diego Zoo, many others throughout the country welcome disabled people and their assistance dogs. This includes zoos in Detroit, Kansas City, the National Zoo in Washington, D.C. and all zoos, wildlife parks and aquaria in Florida. At the Bronx and Philadelphia Zoos, all assistance dogs, including those in training, are welcomed.

Working with the DOJ, we decided to visit the Kansas City Zoo on our April, 1994 trip to Kansas. KC Zoo policy permitted assistance dogs to accompany their disabled partners in most parts of the park.

Previous pages: Toni, a true animal lover, introduced Ed to the pleasures of visiting zoos where they had hands-on experience with a variety of animals.

Several months before our visit, a free-roaming Australian animal exhibit was opened, and officials were unsure about the reaction of dogs to exhibit animals and vice versa. As animal lovers, we want to jeopardize neither the health and well-being of captive animals nor that of our canine teammates. On the other hand, we do not want our civil rights violated based on myths created by those who would deny us access. Therefore, we welcomed the invitation by zoo officials to demonstrate the reality of guide dogs in an innovative zoo setting.

Dr. Wourms, KC Zoo Director, asked two curators to accompany us throughout the grounds. Viewing Ivy and Kirby as possible prey, the lions, tigers and other big cats became active as we walked by. The pandas and primates ignored the presence of our dogs. One bird in the indoor aviary was startled and flew to another part of the enclosure. The exhibit our Goldens most enjoyed was the sea lions. As these marine mammals leaped in and out of their pool, the dogs looked on with envy.

In the eighty-acre Australian area, kangaroos, emus, black swans and sheep are displayed in their natural habitat. There are no barriers between the animals and the public. Visitors are asked to stay on designated paths, but the animals have no such restrictions. As Ivy and Kirby guided us along the paths, they were interested in the strange smells and sights but were not distracted by them. A male kangaroo guarding his harem eyed the dogs with suspicion until he realized they were not a threat. Observing three-legged Kirby's hopping gait, the kangaroos must have wondered why this animal walked like them, but didn't look anything like them!

An emu was far more interested in our friend Diane Anderson's video camera than in our canine partners. The animal most disturbed by our presence was a mother ewe with a newborn lamb. As she stamped her foot and bleated, we tried to reassure her these were sporting, not herding, dogs!

You Can't Bring That Dog in Here

Every one of us partnered with a guide, hearing or service dog dreads being confronted with the words, "You can't bring that dog in here." What is most anxiety-producing about these encounters is their unexpected and random nature.

Try to imagine yourself at work one morning. A new gift shop has opened near your office and you plan to go there during your lunch hour. After work you plan to take a taxi to meet a friend for dinner and a show. During these excursions, you may find the gift shop does not have what you want, the air-conditioning in the taxi is not working, the meal you order is not served hot and the play is a real flop. As disabled people partnered with assistance dogs, we may face all of these problems just as the rest of the population. However, we also are constantly faced with the possible hassles of being refused a ride in the taxi and denied entry to the gift shop, restaurant or theater.

Two blind friends decided to have dinner with a sighted friend in a Kansas City, Missouri, Chinese restaurant. As they entered the Red Dragon with their guide dogs, the proprietor told them to leave their dogs in the lobby outside the dining area. Despite explanations about guide dogs and producing a copy of the state law, the management refused to yield and the three friends left in disgust. They subsequently hired a lawyer and filed charges in civil court.

Usually, faced with legal action, a restaurant owner apologizes, pays a small fine and tries to appease the customers by offering complimentary meals. In this case, however, the restaurant owner hired a lawyer who was ready for combat. During the three years it took for this complaint to be heard in court, Cindy and Bill were emotionally stressed by the tactics of the restaurant's lawyer. In resolving the case, the judge found in favor of Cindy and Bill, awarding them a cash settlement and payment of their legal fees. The final settlement will cost the owner of the Red Dragon more than $25,000 in addition to his own lawyer's charges. That certainly was an expensive dinner!

Another interesting restaurant case took place in St. Louis, Missouri. Marilyn is a service dog trainer, as well as being partnered with a service dog. She had arranged to have dinner with two potential clients at a Cecil Whitaker's restaurant. As she entered with her dog, both a waitress and the manager asked her to leave. Like Bill and Cindy, Marilyn produced a copy of the state law, but the management would not yield. Disregarding the manager's protests, Marilyn joined her clients at their table and began eating the previously ordered food. Knowing the law was on her side, Marilyn suggested the police be called.

To her dismay, the police were unwilling to uphold the law and told Marilyn she must remove the dog from the restaurant. Unbeknownst to Marilyn, a television reporter was having dinner at Whitaker's, observed the incident and featured the story on the evening news. Refusing to be a victim, she filed a complaint with the DOJ citing a violation of her rights under the ADA.

Like other wheelchair users, Rod, a young man from upstate New York, sought partnership with a service dog to improve his level of independence. To his consternation, this choice threatened his financial independence. Employed as a switchboard operator at a community college, Rod was barred from returning to work when he arrived with his new canine partner. A co-worker who ran the switchboard on the earlier shift protested the dog's presence because of her severe allergies. She threatened to file a complaint under the ADA if the administration permitted Rod to bring his dog to the workplace.

Although Rod and his canine assistant had been teamed for only a few weeks, he was unwilling to endanger the bonding process by leaving his dog home. Immediately thrown into an advocacy role, Rod got a lawyer and filed a complaint against his employers. The co-worker was unwilling to yield to any compromise or accommodation. After more than a year of negotiation, the college offered Rod a comparable job in another department where he would be able to bring his dog. However, they have refused to grant back pay for the time he has been barred from the workplace. Rod has accepted the college's offer.

Darlene Sullivan, CEO of Canine Partners for Life, Cochranville, Pennsylvania, reported that a graduate of her program, denied the right to return to his drive-through window job at a New Jersey McDonald's with his service dog, settled for an out-of-court financial arrangement. The money he received from the settlement is being used to pay for his college education. Can we call this a McScholarship?

Wilson, a long-term employee of the President's Committee on the Employment of People with Disabilities, trained with a service dog at National Education Assistance Dog Service (NEADS). A co-worker with a documented dog phobia demanded her right to reasonable accommodation under the ADA. Loosely translated, this meant she did not want Wilson to bring his dog into the office.

Two of the thirty-seven Committee employees already brought their assistance dogs to work with them. The presence of a third dog, she claimed, would trigger her phobia and interfere with her ability to effectively perform her job.

For more than three months until the conflict was resolved, Wilson was not allowed to return to the office. The Committee placed this case of conflicting disability needs in the hands of the Department of Labor. Labor returned the case to the Committee, telling them to make reasonable accommodation for both employees. The final resolution, originally proposed by Wilson at the beginning of the dispute, is for each of the employees with an assistance dog to signal the psychiatrically-disabled employee when the assistance dog team is moving about the building. This will be accomplished by using the existing lighting capacity of the telephone system.

In mid-February 1995 we phoned for a taxi and the driver, seeing Ed's guide dog, refused to take us. We reported the incident to the Fresno City licensing department, and they took immediate action. Their recommendation was to suspend the driver for six months and to take the company's entire fleet of sixteen cabs out of service for thirty days.

The company appealed, and a formal hearing was held in early May. In the one-and-a-half-hour hearing presided over by an administrative judge, the Fresno City Attorney questioned the manager of the licensing department, the owners of the taxi company and us. The owners contended that the Muslim driver was allergic to and fearful of dogs. Ultimately, they claimed the driver's religion prohibited him from transporting dogs and requiring him to do so would constitute religious persecution. The judge was unsympathetic with these excuses, particularly since all Fresno taxi companies were notified two years earlier that both federal and state law prohibit discrimination against disabled people with assistance dogs. At the conclusion of the hearing, the judge's ruling sustained the driver's suspension and called for the thirty-day suspension of four vehicles rather than the entire fleet.

Those of us who encounter access denials may feel frustrated and angry. However, when we take responsibility and pursue these denials in the legal system, the outcome can be personally rewarding and of benefit to the entire community of assistance dog partners.

Chapter Thirteen

Consumerism

In any consumer movement, knowledge and organization are essential elements. The issue of education and choice is being addressed by the publication of books and resource material describing the work performed by our dogs and the various programs training them.

In the organizational arena, an exciting development has been the founding of the International Association of Assistance Dog Partners (IAADP). Throughout this book we have used the term partner to designate our relationship with our assistance dogs. We would welcome the opportunity to use this term in the portrayal of our relationship with the programs providing our canine assistants. A healthy move in that direction has taken place with joint conferences bringing together IAADP and Assistance Dogs International.

A New Consumer Advocacy Organization

On the night of October 6, 1993, an air of excitement and anticipation permeated the atmosphere of the meeting room at the Marriott in St. Louis, Missouri. More than twenty disabled people partnered with assistance dogs entered the room and took their seats. Our goal that night was to create a national cross-disability consumer advocacy group composed of blind people partnered with guide dogs, deaf people partnered with hearing dogs and physically disabled people partnered with service dogs.

Most of the established hearing and service dog training programs are members of Assistance Dogs International, but guide dog programs have not been willing to join. Although only training programs are accorded full voting rights in ADI, many disabled people partnered with assistance dogs have joined as auxiliary members. For the two days preceding the organizational meeting of the

Golden Retrievers Jake and Ivy, Border Collie Noah and Samoyed Nikki, founding dogs of the International Association of Assistance Dog Partners, pose for a portrait.

IAADP, several of us had been circulating flyers and making announcements at the ADI conference.

One of the organizing teams, Joan Froling and service dog Nikki, announced that Paws With a Cause had generously offered us a one-year grant to publish a quarterly newsletter. This newsletter under the editorship of Joan, would, we hoped, become the enticement for joining the organization. It would be geared toward the advocacy goals of IAADP and reflect and give voice to the needs of the membership.

IAADP's first goal would be to notify the 15,000 disabled Americans partnered with assistance dogs about the availability of this publication. A more wide-reaching goal would be spreading the word to an international disabled audience.

Based upon the ensuing discussion of IAADP's goals, we delineated four major overlapping themes. These were education, legislation, advocacy and mutual support.

We all agreed education would be a primary focus. Despite the presence of guide dogs in the United States for sixty years, many people do not know what they do for their blind partners. Since hearing and service dogs were unknown until twenty years ago, an even larger segment of the population is unaware of the role they play in the lives of their disabled partners. If the general public is unaware of the benefits of working with assistance dogs, so is a large segment of the disabled community. In addition, we need to educate each other about the work our dogs do for us and our disability-related needs. Surprisingly, many guide dog handlers have little knowledge of the functions of hearing and service dogs, and many blind people have little knowledge about the impact of deafness and physical disabilities on the lives of their disabled peers. The same could equally be said about those who are deaf and those who are physically disabled.

Although most consumer organizations do not take an explicitly active legislative and lobbying function, those attending this initial meeting thought we needed to overtly recognize our political role in fostering the rights of our canine partners to accompany us in all places open to the public. Attempts have been made to restrict these rights and we need to be vigilant to make sure they are not curtailed in the future. An additional legislative thrust intends to improve and extend the protection we currently enjoy.

Although participation in the political process might assure legal rights, the realities of everyday life do not always conform to the law. All those at the meeting had faced situations in which their legal access rights were denied. In some cases, individuals do not know

Hearing dog Noah enjoys a magic moment with partner Ilene Caroom, an IAADP founding Board Member.
Dan Beigel

their rights. In other situations, we need the support of our peers to help us fight against those who would keep us out of their taxis, hotels, motels, restaurants, theaters, shopping malls, medical offices

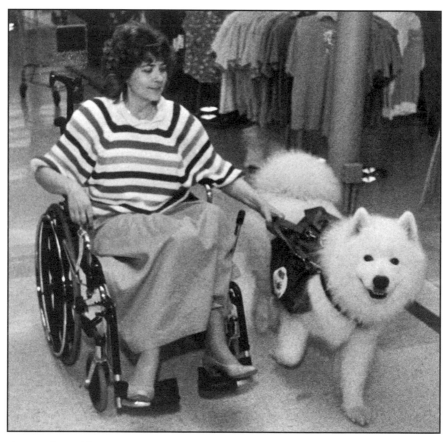

Service dog Nikki assists partner Joan Froling on a shopping trip. Joan is IAADP Board Chairperson and editor of Partners' Forum. Courtesy of Joan Froling

and numerous other locations in which we would be warmly welcomed—without our assistance dogs.

A major advocacy goal identified by the group was the development of programs to help maintain the partnership and continue the bond. If we think of the tightly-knit partnership between us and our canine teammates, the cement that helps maintain the bond is the care delivered by veterinarians. When our dogs go through major health crises, the costs involved may be so large as to impoverish the human partner or force a premature breaking of the bond. We need to advocate for our dogs in such crises. In addition to working with veterinarians, we need to work with drug and dog food manufacturers and others to take some of the financial burden off those least able to bear it. Disabled people are particularly vulnerable because of the high levels of unemployment and impoverishment faced by many of them.

A wide range of activities was suggested under the goal of mutual support. One was to share information about training, dog care, equipment, disease and disease control. Another was to share information locally about veterinarians, obedience trainers and other professionals providing products and services required by our dogs. Recognition was given to the need for providing information about existing programs so those considering canine partnership can make informed choices. A final support area discussed was related to relieving grief at the breaking of the bond. For all of us who have gone through this traumatic experience, having the support of others who realize the depths of our loss has been very helpful.

One Year Later

In August 1994 in Washington, D.C., IAADP again met in conjunction with ADI. IAADP's board of directors presented a panel for ADI discussing the reasons for a consumer coalition and the needed partnership between the two organizations.

The major accomplishment of the previous year was the publication of two issues of an outstanding newsletter under the inspired editorship of Joan Froling. She proudly reported our subscriber mailing list exceeded 1,000 and was growing rapidly. Acknowledging the generous grant from Paws with a Cause to publish *Partners' Forum* would run out at the end of 1994, meeting participants brainstormed

IAADP Board Member Jean Levitt is assisted by her service dog Cole in a wide variety of daily situations. Jean Levitt

about future funding sources. Time was set aside to discuss the future structure of the organization.

Despite the protection provided by the ADA and state laws, we are still faced with access problems when accompanied by our assistance dogs. We chose as our first year's national objective the education of taxi drivers about our right to ride in their cabs. Drivers are frequently unaware assistance dogs are quiet, clean and well-mannered. Many in the audience related that after convincing reluctant drivers to take them, the cabbies often comment that assistance dogs are better behaved than some human passengers!

New Yorker Jean Levitt, teamed with Cole, a Rough Collie service dog, described her campaign to teach taxi drivers to recognize assistance dogs and better understand their role in the lives of their disabled partners. Jean assumed responsibility for the preparation of an access brochure to be published in a future issue of *Partners' Forum*.

Kathy Hurst, former Executive Director of Top Dog, volunteered to work with IAADP in developing a certification program. Although ADI is working toward a uniform, standardized test of assistance dog/disabled person teams to be administered by training programs for their graduates, no provision has been made for certifying non-program trained teams. Several dogs in the audience, including Toni's guide Ivy, had been privately trained, either by their disabled partners or by private trainers hired for this purpose. Although the ADA does not require proof of certification, IAADP and ADI agree a performance standard would make the public feel more secure about legitimate teams having access rights. In addition, all ADI member programs would strive for the same standard of excellence and private trainers would conform to a similar standard. The group liked Kathy's ideas and asked her to submit a written proposal.

The featured speaker at the joint banquet was Bob Williams, Commissioner for the Administration on Developmental Disabilities. Bob is the highest ranking official in President Bill Clinton's administration partnered with an assistance dog. Decoy, his yellow Labrador service dog, is a graduate of Canine Partners for Life. Bob's speech, delivered by means of the Liberator speech board, was easily understood.

Access Brochure

One of the unanticipated events in the short history of IAADP was the selection of *Partners' Forum* as a 1994 nominee by the Dog Writers Association of America (DWAA). In February, 1995 we traveled to New York to attend the DWAA annual banquet. In addition to *Partners' Forum*, our column, "Partners in Independence," as well as "Kirby's Miracle," a feature article in *Fetch the Paper*, received award nominations.

While in New York, we met with Jean Levitt, who organized a photo session to illustrate the taxi access brochure she was preparing for IAADP. Wonder of wonders, she and her son Barry commandeered a New York City taxi driver willing to take part in this project. Photos were taken showing Jean and Cole getting in and out of his taxi. This wonderfully cooperative New York City taxi driver from India was quick to point out that he was only driving a taxi until he could take and pass the licensing examinations permitting him to resume his career as a medical doctor. Although he spent over half an hour with our "film crew," he refused financial compensation for his time. A rare New York City taxi driver indeed!

Two Years Later

We set our alarm clock for 6 A.M. to make our overseas call. With the eight-hour difference between California and England, we wanted to ensure that we would reach the Guide Dogs for the Blind Association during office hours. Paul Master, Director of Operations, was scheduled to attend the joint meetings of ADI and IAADP to be held in Las Vegas in September, 1995. With great expectations, we invited him to be the banquet speaker. To our chagrin, his immediate reaction was to politely decline the invitation. Responding to our obvious disappointment, Paul said he would give it some thought and let us know in a day or so. When his call came a day later, we were delighted and relieved by his acceptance of the invitation.

Given the diversity within the assistance dog movement, ADI's purpose is to bring training organizations together in a common forum. Among its accomplishments to date are the establishment of a code of ethics for member programs, setting minimum standards for training both dogs and students, promoting legislation protecting the rights of disabled people accompanied by assistance dogs and exchanging information about equipment and fundraising activities.

Although we had never met Paul, he had been instrumental in arranging for our trips to the U.K. in 1989 and 1990 to do comparative research on the guide dog movement in our respective countries. We were delighted when Paul and his wife Sheila joined us for dinner the night before the conference began. On Monday night Paul joined our IAADP panel on access issues. He provided a general picture of acceptance of guide dog partners and their dogs in public places in the U.K. Comparing the U.K. and U.S., he noted the lack of legal recourse available to guide dog partners facing access denials in his country. GDBA, working with and on behalf of their graduates, uses persuasion rather than legal remedies. However, Paul noted considerable problems still occur in the realms of taxis and restaurants. Members of the audience were quick to note that, despite the existence of legal protection in the U.S., similar problems also exist here.

Following Paul's discussion, members of the IAADP board presented several skits about access denials. In one of our favorites titled "You can't bring *that* dog in here," Ed played a restaurant manager while Toni entered with Nikki, Joan's Samoyed service dog. After being told by Ed that she couldn't bring *that* dog in the restaurant,

Toni apologized and left. She then returned with Escort, her Golden guide dog and said, "I know you didn't like *that* dog, but how about *this* one?" That skit really brought the house down.

During the two nights of IAADP meetings, Joan and other board members reported on recent activities. *Partners' Forum*, fulfilling our expectations, has become a major vehicle enabling those of us with disabilities to express ourselves and discuss basic concerns about working with canine partners.

Newly-elected board member Jean Levitt's access brochure was published in the Summer 1995 issue of the *Forum*. It has been a major breakthrough. The brochure can be readily reproduced, and the pictures on the front can be replaced by photos of any team. Individuals facing access confrontations reported the almost magical quality of this brochure which contains its basic message in Punjabi, Urdu, Chinese, Spanish, French and English. Access rights and the penalties for denial of access are delineated.

For us, the highlight of the conference was the banquet presentation. Paul outlined the history and goals of the International Federation of Guide Dog Schools, a world-wide coalition of guide dog training programs. He formally announced the application for membership in the Federation for the first two U.S. schools, Guide Dogs of America and Guide Dogs for the Blind. Moving on to a discussion of Dogs for the Disabled U.K., he described GDBA's role in fostering that program. Finally, Paul spoke about Assistance Dogs U.K., the British equivalent of ADI. To the delight of the audience of more than 100 people, he ended his presentation by donning a Las Vegas cap to symbolize his commitment to return to next year's ADI/IAADP conference.

Chapter Fourteen

Let's Laugh

One of the unique aspects of the human condition is our ability to laugh at ourselves. People with disabilities, like many others, find reasons to laugh all around them. Sometimes the humor is directly related to the disabling condition, sometimes not. As members of that small minority of disabled people choosing to work with assistance dogs, we find a great deal of amusement in encounters with the public in which our dogs are essential ingredients.

Ed and Kirby, Toni and Ivy visit Disneyland in Anaheim, California where Donald Duck and Mickey Mouse greet them with a true VIP welcome. Courtesy of Disneyland

"Out of Sight Guide Dog" School

While sitting at our kitchen table one day, we began to make up silly descriptions of guide dog schools. We had recently completed our book about these organizations and were full of ideas. Features of the schools noted in our book included their charitable nature, the student-dog matching process, the breeds used and the necessity of going to a school for a month and being isolated from family and friends as a result.

Having inundated ourselves in these details, we began speculating about a way-out type of guide dog school. The result of these somewhat goofy speculations was the "Out of Sight Guide Dog" concept. What follows is a notice to blind people about the unique features of our mythical school.

> Have you hesitated about getting a guide dog because they are so big? Are you a guide dog partner who has trouble getting your large dog under a table in a restaurant or under the seat in buses and subways? Are people always tripping over your dog? We have solved your problem. "Out of Sight," our new school, will provide you with a dog who can fit anywhere. Our breed, pocket Poodles, will never be obtrusive. As a Toy breed, they never weigh more than three pounds. Thus, they can be carried in pocket, purse, backpack, special pouch or even in one's hand. Since they are so portable, they need never touch the floor. Therefore, you do not have to worry about tripping over them and never have to wipe their feet or remove gum from their coats.

> Are you afraid that if you get a guide dog you will be eaten out of house and home? Do you have backaches because of carrying tons of food when you travel with your guide dog? A five-pound bag of dog food will feed our dogs for six months.

> Are you reluctant to get a guide dog because you like to sleep late on your days off? Do you resent your present guide dog because you have to put on your winter clothes and take your dog out into the freezing air on a day when you are not going anywhere? Have you had to buy stock

in the Baggies™ company due to the necessity of picking up after your dog? All of these problems disappear with our dogs. They are trained to relieve in a litter pan. You do not have to go outdoors unless you want to.

Do you think twice about getting a guide dog because you have heard there are problems getting into public places with your dog? Have you ever had a taxi driver, restaurant owner, theater operator or hotel proprietor challenge your right to keep your guide dog with you? Are you tired of hearing, "You can't bring that dog in here?" Your problems are over. Our dogs are so small they are rarely seen. In the event you are challenged, just slip your dog out of sight. You can then reply, "What dog?"

Have you rejected the idea of getting a guide dog because you don't want to leave your family to spend a month at a school some distance from your home? At our school we invite you and your entire family to spend a week having fun in the sun while you train. In one short week you can learn to work with a pocket Poodle. Training is simple. You carry your dog in your hand. If the dog wiggles to the left, you turn left; if the dog wiggles to the right, you turn right; when the dog lifts his nose in the air, you stop since you are at a curb or obstacle. If the dog puts her nose down, you are at the top of a staircase. The most complicated part of the training program is learning how to deftly slip your dog out of sight into your pocket.

While in training, you and your family are invited to spend a luxurious week at the Hawaii Coconut Pineapple Lodge. Rooms are deluxe, meals are delicious and every recreational facility is within easy reach. Between training sessions you and your family may want to spend time on the beach.

In our scientific matching process, you enter the hotel banquet room barefoot and the first of the five hundred specially trained pocket Poodles to lick your toes becomes your guide dog. One of the major innovative ideas in guide dog ideology is the concept that the dog should select you.

Scientific studies have clearly demonstrated this procedure drastically reduces the number of poor matches.

Another feature of our school is the provision of aftercare anywhere in the continental United States. Should you, for any reason, have to return to our school in Hawaii, do not fear the quarantine. After all, your dog is out of sight.

We are thinking of establishing a mandatory annual walk-a-thon reunion to raise funds for your alma mater. However, there are some logistical problems. The most significant one is the mass smuggling of vast numbers of pocket Poodle guide dogs into Hawaii.

Who is eligible to receive an "Out of Sight Guide Dog"? Any blind person who can contribute $50,000 or more is eligible to receive one of our dogs. The school, as a charitable trust, will pay all travel, hotel, meals and entertainment expenses for you and your family. We will also provide a healthy, well-trained "Out of Sight Guide Dog." You do not have to walk fast or have good balance.

What are some of the other advantages of our dogs? Small dogs, as we all know, live longer than big dogs. Often our large guide dogs must be retired when they develop arthritis. However, since you carry your "Out of Sight Guide Dog" in your hand, this is not a problem. You need never worry about sniffing, scavenging or chasing other dogs.

Our dogs are taught to fetch on command. They are willing workers, but heavy wallets and key chains may be too much for them. However, they are fantastic at fetching bobby pins and toothpicks.

Despite the phenomenal success of our new concept, we must recognize certain disadvantages. With larger dogs you may have the painful experience of having them step on your feet. With our guide dogs, should you step on them, a successor may be necessary. Another problem is cats. Your "Out of Sight" dog has been trained to get along with cats. However, if the cat mistakes your dog for a mouse, an immediate successor may be in order.

Shaggy Guide Dog Stories

We're sure you have all heard the story of the blind man who enters a large department store and twirls his guide dog around his head. When a startled salesperson asks if he needs help, he replies, "No thank you; I'm only looking around!" And there's the question: "Why don't blind people sky dive?" The answer, of course, is "Their guide dogs would get too nervous!!" Most guide dog partners do not find these frequently told stories funny. On the other hand, real life situations can be much funnier.

Daisy and her Australian Shepherd guide dog, Outback, boarded a nonstop flight from New York to Los Angeles. After three hours in the air, a flight attendant asked what would happen if Outback needed to relieve herself during the flight. Daisy responded in a serious tone, "The pilot would have to land the plane." Quite startled, the attendant replied, "I'm so sorry. That simply can't be done!"

Rob was daydreaming as he and his Labrador Retriever guide dog, Flint, strolled down a street in Brooklyn, New York. Flint stopped at the curb as guide dogs are trained to do and Rob listened to the flow of traffic. When the parallel traffic began moving, he knew the light was in his favor. Caught up in his reverie, Rob gave his Forward in a less than commanding tone. Flint, busy sniffing a pole, ignored him. Rob repeated the command in a slightly firmer voice. Flint continued to sniff. Realizing the light would turn against him in a moment, Rob raised his voice and delivered the Forward in a more authoritative tone. Flint snapped to attention and smartly guided Rob across the street. Stepping onto the up curb, he overheard one lady say to another, "What a shame, Sadie, a blind man with a deaf dog!"

Karl was in an unfamiliar part of Chicago when his Boxer guide dog, Dempsey, indicated he needed to visit the curb. After Dempsey had finished defecating, Carl picked up using a plastic bag. Karl then began searching along the curb for a trash bin. A passing motorist directed him to a container a few feet to his left. It was only at the last moment, as Carl lifted the lid, that he realized the well-intentioned (?) motorist had directed him to a U.S. mailbox. Fortunately for the mail carrier, Karl realized the mistake in time!

As Rosie and her German Shepherd guide dog, Greta, waited for a train on a subway platform in Philadelphia, a curious bystander approached them and asked, "Will your dog let you know which train pulls in?" "She will now," Rosie replied. Confused by this response, the bystander inquired, "Why now? Did you have problems with your dog in the past?" Rosie, sensing the gullibility of her questioner, continued, "I certainly did. You see, my dog Greta is a German Shepherd. When I first got her, I did not speak a word of German. I remedied this by taking a night course in German and we communicate quite well, now!" "How wonderful!" exclaimed the bystander. She must have had a great story to tell her family that night.

While on vacation at a seaside resort in Florida, Arnold allowed his guide dog, Darla to run free. True to her Golden Retriever heritage, Darla was stimulated by her surroundings. As Arnold sunned himself on the pier, he heard a splash followed by raucous laughter from his friends. Apparently the temptation to swim had been too much for Darla and she launched herself off the pier into the water. Suddenly, the laughter turned to gasps of surprise. Darla had spotted a snorkeler and was heading straight toward him. Her curiosity aroused, she approached him in a few powerful strokes. Realizing this strange apparition was merely another human being, she placed her paws on his shoulders, licked his face mask and turned toward shore. Imagine the snorkeler's shock at this unexpected invasion of his watery wonderland!

Peggy and her date were to dine at an expensive Detroit restaurant. Of course, Midnight, Peggy's black German Shepherd guide dog, made it a threesome. While waiting for their table, they went into the bar for a drink. Set up for romantic trysts, the bar was quite dark. Midnight lay alongside Peggy's bar stool, since there was no table under which she could go. A slightly inebriated man sitting nearby noticed the dark object on the ground and attempted to retrieve it. With an exclamation of utter terror, he blurted out, "My God, it's alive! I thought you dropped your fur coat."

On a freezing cold morning in Baltimore, Jim harnessed his Doberman Pinscher guide dog, Sandy, and walked to his waiting taxi. It didn't take much to persuade the taxi driver to stop for a cup of coffee at a nearby convenience store. "Sandy and I will get the coffee," offered Jim. "It's not necessary for you to come in with me." Thankful not to have to face the cold, the taxi driver buried his head in his newspaper. Clutching the bag containing the two cups of coffee in his gloved hand, Jim told Sandy to find the taxi. She threaded her way past several cars in the parking lot and stopped at the door of one. Praising Sandy's cleverness, they hopped into the car and Jim closed the door. When Jim reached forward and attempted to give the cup to the driver, Jim realized something was drastically wrong. His hand encountered a Plexiglas divider that had not been there five minutes before. Realizing this was not his taxi, Jim tried to get out, but there were no door handles. Meanwhile, the taxi driver realized something was wrong and went into the store looking for his fare. The cashier remembered chatting with Jim about Sandy just a few minutes before. Overhearing the conversation, two police officers wished the taxi driver luck in finding Jim and Sandy. As they approached their car, they let out a victory hoot. They had discovered Jim and Sandy locked in the back of their sound-proof, escape-proof patrol car!

Appendix A

Tips on Being Disability Cool

When interacting with a disabled person, maintain eye contact, offer to shake hands and relate directly to the person with a disability, rather than with a nondisabled companion. Relax! Don't be embarrassed if you use common disability-related expressions such as "See you later," "I've got to be running along" or "Have you heard about that."

Most disabling conditions do not impair the ability to think, plan or make decisions, so do not treat disabled people like children or attempt to take control away from them. Do not intrude by asking personal questions you would not ask other strangers or new acquaintances. Asking about the cause, duration or prognosis of the disabling condition may be considered presumptuous.

It's acceptable to offer assistance to a person with a disability, but wait until your offer is accepted before you help. Listen to and follow the directions provided by the disabled person. Don't be offended if your offer of help is declined.

When talking with a person in a wheelchair, pull up a chair if possible so you are at eye level. This puts you on an equal footing and avoids neck strain for both of you. Do not lean on or attempt to push the wheelchair. This may be viewed as an invasion of personal space. Although a person seated in a wheelchair may be at the same height as a child, resist the patronizing temptation to pat him/her on the head or shoulder.

When greeting a blind person, always identify yourself and others who may be with you. When conversing in a group, remember to identify the person to whom you are speaking. Speak in a normal tone of voice, indicate when you move from one place to another, and let the blind person know when you are leaving. When you offer to assist a person with a visual disability, offer your arm so the person may be guided, not propelled, by you.

To get the attention of a person with a hearing disability, tap her/him on the shoulder or wave your hand. Look directly at the individual and speak clearly, slowly and expressively. Not all persons with hearing disabilities are lip readers. Those who are rely on facial expression and other body language to help them understand. It is considerate to place yourself facing the light source, and keep your hands, food and smoking materials away from your mouth. Shouting won't help; writing notes will.

Give your full attention when communicating with persons with speech impairments. Be patient, and do not try to complete sentences or speak for them. When necessary, ask short questions requiring short answers, a nod or a shake of the head. Never pretend to understand if you are having difficulty doing so. Repeat what you think you heard, and look for clarification from the disabled person.

Whether wearing a harness, backpack, vest or other identifying equipment, an assistance dog is on duty. Just as you should not interfere with a human concentrating on a task, you should never interrupt the work of an assistance dog.

Although you may be a dog lover and assistance dogs are extremely appealing, don't pet, talk to or feed them without receiving permission from the human partner. Petting, whistling at or talking to a working dog may distract him and disorient or endanger the disabled teammate. Feeding an assistance dog may disrupt a carefully controlled feeding schedule and cause the dog to become ill. Dogs who learn to accept unauthorized food handouts may become unruly beggars when accompanying their disabled partners in public places where food is served.

Do not be offended if the disabled person declines your friendly overtures. He may be in a hurry and not have time to stop. She may be shy or reserved and may not enjoy interacting with strangers. On the other hand, the disabled person may welcome the opportunity to chat. Throughout this book we have described the role of assistance dogs as social icebreakers. Many disabled people enjoy this added dimension of the partnership, while others do not.

Appendix B

Assistance Dog Resources Cited in This Book

Space does not permit a complete listing of all the assistance dog training programs. Therefore, only those mentioned in the text are cited here. Listings followed by TT refer to the presence of text telephones permitting direct communication with deaf and individuals who are hard of hearing. For further information about assistance dog partnerships, please contact:

Assistance Dogs International
Mike Roche, President
980 Everett Street
Lakewood, CO 80215
(303) 234-9512

The Delta Society
Service Dog Resource Center
289 Perimeter Road East
Renton, WA 98055
(800) 869-6898 Ext. 16 (Voice)
(800) 809-2714 (TT)

International Association of
    Assistance Dog Partners
PO Box 1326
Sterling Heights, MI 48311
(810) 826-3938

The following are Assistance Dog Training Programs:

Canine Companions for
   Independence
PO Box 446
Santa Rosa, CA 95402
(800) 572-2275 or
(707) 577-1700

Canine Partners for Life
130D RD 2
Cochranville, PA 19330
(610) 869-4902

Dogs for the Deaf
10175 Wheeler Road
Central Point, OR 97502
(800) 990-3647 or
(503) 826-9220

Fidelco Guide Dog Foundation
PO Box 142
Bloomfield, CT 06002
(860) 243-5200

Freedom Service Dogs Inc.
980 Everett Street
Lakewood, CO 80215
(303) 234-9512

Guide Dog Foundation for the Blind
371 East Jericho Turnpike
Smithtown, NY 11787
(800) 548-4337 or
(516) 265-2121

Guide Dogs for the Blind
   Association
Hillfields Burghfield Common
Reading, Berks. RG7 3YG England
(01144) 0734-835555 (phone)

Guide Dogs for the Blind Inc.
PO Box 151200
San Rafael, CA 94915
(800) 295-4050 or
(415) 499-4000

Guide Dogs of America
13445 Glenoaks Boulevard
Sylmar, CA 91342
(818) 362-5834

Guide Dogs of the Desert
PO Box 1692
Palm Springs, CA 92263
(619) 329-6257

Guiding Eyes for the Blind
611 Granite Springs Road
Yorktown Heights, NY 10598
(800) 942-0149 or
(914) 245-4024

Happy Canine Helpers Inc.
16277 Montgomery Road
Johnstown, OH 43031
(614) 965-2204

International Hearing Dog Inc.
5901 East 89 Avenue
Henderson, CO 80640
(303) 287-3277

Israel Guide Dog Center
   for the Blind
Beit Oved 76800 Israel
(011972) 08-408-213 (phone)

Kansas Specialty Dog Service
PO Box 216
Washington, KS 66968
(913) 325-2256

Leader Dogs for the Blind
PO Box 5000
Rochester, MI 48308
(810) 651-9011

National Education for Assistance
   Dog Services
(formerly New England Assistance
   Dog Service)
PO Box 213
Boylston, MA 01583
(508) 422-9064

Okada Ltd.
W5634 Sterns Road
Fontana, WI 53125
(414) 275-5226

Paws With a Cause
4646 South Division
Wayland, MI 49348
(800) 253-7297

Pilot Dogs Inc.
625 West Town Street
Columbus, OH 43215
(614) 221-6367

Prison Pet Partnership Program
PO Box 17
Gig Harbor, WA 98335
(206) 858-9101 Ext. 240

San Francisco SPCA Hearing
   Dog Program
2500 16 Street
San Francisco, CA 94103
(415) 554-3020 (Voice)
(415) 554-3022 (TT)

Southeastern Guide Dogs
4210 77 Street East
Palmetto, FL 33561
(941) 729-5665

Texas Hearing and Service Dogs
4803 Rutherglen
Austin TX 78749
(512) 891-9090

The Seeing Eye™
PO Box 375
Morristown, NJ 07960
(800) 539-4425 or
(201) 539-4425

Top Dog
5315 East Broadway Suite 105
Tucson, AZ 85711
(602) 747-4945